M000196311

FASTIING

VOLUME II

YOUR LIFE AS A WEAPON
IN THE HAND OF GOD

MICHAEL DOW

BURNING ONES
PUBLISHING

ACKNOWLEDGMENTS

Thank you to my wife, Anna, and four beautiful children: Ariyah, Josiah, Emma, and Isaiah. I love you more than I know how to say. The joy you bring to my life has immeasurably enriched who I am as a person. I am grateful for you beyond words and thank the Lord for the push you continually give me because of the way you believe in me.

Thank you to our Burning Ones team. All of you are without a doubt a gift from God. You have stood next to me, believed in me, and carried me through some of my most significant moments in life, both publicly and privately. I honor each of you and the wonderful place that God has put you in my heart and my family's life.

Thank you to Kathy Curtis, who has been such a treasure from the Lord during the process of helping me get my books together over the years. Your excellence and humility are second to none.

Thank you to Omar Galarza for the incredible cover design for this book project. Omar, I am grateful to God that He has put us together. You and your wife are family to us.

Thank you for all of you who over the years have impacted my life in this conversation of fasting. Whether you realize it or not, you have played a significant role in who I am today. The forming of the image of Jesus in my life has been aggressively accelerated because of the One that I have found out in the deep. He constantly beckons to me. His voice stirs deep within my soul, and it has been one of the great joys of my life to be sensitive and responsive to Him in the place of fasting and prayer. I honor all of you who have impacted me because of what it has produced in me, more of Him! May we continue on with great grace and glory.

DEDICATION

I dedicate this book to all of the hungry travelers on the pathway of consecration and brokenness in this life that leads to more of Jesus. Don't ever buy into the lie that you have had enough; there is more. There is more than you ever thought. There is more than your wildest imagination can contain. There is more because He is endless and inexhaustible. There is more because He Himself is an ever-unfolding and ever-increasing revelation. It will take us all of eternity to enjoy the explorative process of the depths of knowing Him.

May you find yourself completely immersed into the depths of Jesus. May you willingly and joyfully dive headfirst into Him and never look back. This is not a matter of the mind; it is the response of the heart. Reason will lie to you and tell you that you have already found enough to be satisfied. Fleshly reason will attempt to hold you back by swallowing the lie that you have already tasted and seen *enough*. But to that, I tell you that there is more! Oh, precious one that hungers after Jesus and the real experience of His person. O taste and see that the Lord is good![1]

All of you for all of Him. All of Him for all of you. This is my prayer for you as I dedicate this book to you, the hungry traveler. Continue on. Keep pressing. Keep asking. Keep seeking. Keep knocking. And may He be opened up to you. As you turn your natural appetite over to Him, may He wonderfully and gloriously fill you time and time again. He is good, and worthy of this pursuit. He waits to be wanted. He wants to be wanted. He is the rewarder of those who seek Him.

---

[1] Ps 34:8

TABLE OF CONTENTS

PROLOGUE

The great need in our day is for people to set their gaze purely upon the person of Jesus. Too many other things have glistened and dazzled the attention of our hearts off of purely being fascinated and obsessed with Jesus, just for Jesus. People want Jesus so that they can use their love for Jesus to work their way into other things. This must come to an end. We must love Him for Him. We must come to Him for Him, and Him alone.

He is better and more fulfilling than all of the secondary and supplemental items, that at times if we are not careful, eclipse the attention of our hearts and sit higher in priority than just Him and Him alone.

Even though this situation that I am describing to you may sound tragic, in the midst of it there are a people rising in the earth. There are a people who are coming to the forefront. They are wild. They are free.

They are madly in love. And they are not concerned with the other things that this life may have to offer for they have secured all they had ever hoped and longed for in Jesus.

There are a people coming with burning hearts. Hearts ablaze for the King and His Kingdom, and they cannot be stopped. They cannot be stopped for they have joyfully chosen to deny themselves and follow after Him, for Him. They cannot be defeated for they have willingly lost all things in Him and for His glory alone.

We must love Him for Him. We must come to Him for Him, and Him alone.

They cannot be ignored for they have gained the audience with a King, and His smile over their lives is all that they live for. The world no longer holds their attention for they have pledged their full allegiance to King Jesus and seeing His Kingdom come!

Oh, yes, these bright ones, these shining stars in the midst of the darkness, they are coming. The day has come that has placed a demand on such a people being necessary to rise, and God is doing it. God seeks a people that will give Him their yes to burn for Him, and these radiant ones offer it to the Lover of their souls in total abandon. They are rebels to the status quo. They are surrendered to God yet uncontrollable to the manipulative efforts of man. They are wild, and they are free!

There are a people coming who will not be satisfied by the spotlight of man because they are living in the light of God. They will not care about finding their joy and satisfaction in the appreciation of the masses because their heart and soul will have been overwhelmed by the love of the One. Their ear will be deafened to the applause of many because it will be fine-tuned to the empowering of God's voice alone and His counsel.

There is a breed of Jesus lovers arising who will care more about pleasing God than about pleasing donors. A people are arising who are not jockeying to find their significance in a public place because God has apprehended them in the secret place. A people who recognize that a secret call to fasting and prayer requires no microphone, no platform. A people coming who could care less about being included in the country club of ministry, business, or politics because they have found their value and delight in being identified with Him.

The world no longer holds their attention for they have pledged their full allegiance to King Jesus and seeing His Kingdom come!

These ones are full of purity and power, declaration and demonstration, revelation and unction. They are weapons of mass destruction in the hands of God, tearing down strongholds, uprooting plans that the enemy attempts to sow into the earth, and shielding off fiery darts from the intentions of the wicked one. They will loose the desires of God into the earth in full measure and manifest glory. Oh, how we desperately need and long for such ones to arise in our day!

Can you hear it? Can you hear the whisper of God into the deepest place of your heart and soul… awaken…come fully alive in Me…it's time!

INTRODUCTION

The end of the age will reveal something to us that I believe will be very startling for some. It will reveal countless men and women that will stand before Jesus, bright shining like the sun, radiant in a glorious splendor. They will beam with an illuminating glow only made possible by the One who is Light filling everything about them. These incandescent ones will enter into their reward, honored by Jesus, for the way that they gave their life to Him fully surrendered as an offering of obedient worship.

I know that you believe this. I know that you wholeheartedly would agree that there is a day of reward coming for those who have been entrusted with the opportunity to lay their lives down in loving surrender to the Lamb that sits up on the throne. What I think will be surprising to us is not that Jesus will honor people, but rather those whom Jesus chooses to honor.

The selection of saints that Jesus chooses to honor is what will take us by surprise.

The reason this will be surprising is that it will undoubtedly be people we have never heard of. There will be an army of lovers Jesus will smile over that were never talked about in great public debate or conversation. It will be a multitude of faithful ones that never had their picture on an advertisement for an event. They were never on television. You may have never had the opportunity to hear their voice on the radio. And the reason for this is because they were never invited. They may have never had the chance to hold a microphone, for that wasn't their ambitious desire or their assignment.

No, no, no, none of these will be honored for those reasons. For in much of the way that the world honors men and women today, these precious saints would have never even made it into the consideration for such things. Their reward will not be determined by the star power of their life, or the applause that their gift was able to generate from crowds.

These will be saints that had a special place in the heart of Jesus. These will be saints that were faithful to Him in secret. Many in hiddenness and obscurity. Many in deep brokenness and sweet, tender surrender in private. Not for résumé building. Not for accolades and awards. Just simply for Jesus, and for Him to be glorified through the yielding of their hearts to His desires. Completely unknown to the world, yet powerfully known by Jesus, and He awaits them on that great day.

This world is not our home. You very easily read over such a statement, because if you have any time at all invested into walking with Jesus or attending church, then you have heard this stated a time or two. However many times it may be that you have heard this statement stated, preached, or prayed, the sensitivity of our hearts must never lose touch with the potency that such a truth has to change our lives.

Eternity will be revealed to us, and then forever and ever and ever we will live to enjoy the One that now, in an immediate way, we have committed our lives to.

This world is not our home. This life is not it for us. There is more. It is coming. No matter what you think about that now, or how you may be living to prepare for that now, it is going to happen. Eternity will be revealed to us, and then forever and ever and ever we will live to enjoy the One that now, in an immediate way, we have committed our lives to.

The danger in not fully grasping that this world is not our home is that if we are not careful, we can get wrapped up into things that only matter right now.

Things that don't have an eternal reward attached to them. We weary ourselves and spin our wheels for things that provide us instant gratification, immediate benefits, temporary rewards. Our lives are pointed towards eternity; we will spend forever with Jesus.

Our lives are not meant to be absorbed into this life so much so that we parade around like the rest of the world around us that must have stardom, influence, power, fame, riches, etc., now, because they are not living with the same hope that we have. At the end of their life they will have already enjoyed what was the best time that they knew, but for you, and for me, this is not the case. At your last breath, you will just be getting started. The best is actually yet to come.

At your last breath, you will just be getting started. The best is actually yet to come.

There is a beautiful section in Hebrews chapter 11 that I love. It reads this way, "All these died in faith, without receiving the promises, but having seen them and having welcomed them from a distance and having confessed that they were strangers and exiles on the earth. For those who say such things make it clear that they are seeking a country of their own. And indeed, if they had been thinking of that country from which they went out, they would have had opportunity to return. But as it is, they desire a better country, that is, a heavenly one. Therefore, God is not ashamed to be their God; for He has prepared a city for them."[2]

God is not ashamed to be their God. Whose God? The God of all of those who have abandoned what is found in this life, realizing that this is not their home, in search of what God has prepared for them. Those who have set their anchor down into the person of Jesus in such a real and deep way that has now formed an allegiance to the promises of God and not simply a desire for this life and what it is able to offer.

These precious ones, who for the sake of what they have seen in Him, have forsaken all other liars and lesser lovers of this present life that seek to bind and distract. God is not ashamed to be their God. No, He is not at all ashamed.

The end of the age will reveal faithful saints that gave their lives over to Jesus in the secret place of fasting and prayer. We may never know their names now, but they also don't live to be known or for some temporary tangible reward. You see, once we put our anchor down in the person of Jesus and are freed from the immediacy of the world around us and all of its sparkling lights and glistening rewards, we can live for things that are ultimate and not just what may be immediate.

---

[2] Heb 11:13-16, NASB

This is not to say that some things that are immediate don't also have connected to them an eternal element, but this is just to speak to the trap of forsaking what is ultimate for the lesser, which is immediate. The world's reward and heaven's reward are not always the same thing. What heaven applauds may not generate the applause of men and women. This is why you must live within your heart, free enough to, like the apostle Paul said, "be obedient to the heavenly vision."[3]

What heaven applauds may not generate the applause of men and women.

Many have given their live to Jesus in the place of fasting and prayer over the generations and seen God do incredible things. Lives have been changed. Cities have been shaken. Regions have been transformed. Countless people have been delivered from death. Kingdoms conquered, other established, and yet others preserved. It is undeniable that God has used men and women throughout the history of the world in the place of fasting and prayer to advance the Kingdom and see His desires fulfilled in the earth.

Some we know because the Scriptures testify of their lives, like Moses, Elijah, Ezra, Esther, Daniel,

---

[3] Acts 26:19, NASB

Joel, Jonah, John the baptizer, Paul the apostle, Jesus, and more. Others will remain unnamed until that great and glorious day when they enter into their reward. Whether known or unknown, many have been faithful. Whether rewarded in an immediate sense or not, many have given their lives over and seen God perform signs, wonders, and miracles.

It is easy to think that fasting and praying is something that doesn't reap much of an immediate reward. This may be the belief of the casual onlooker. But to those of us who have the Holy Spirit and are possessed with a vision of the age to come, you realize that there is much ground to take in the here and now through fasting and praying.

Let others criticize and ridicule if they want to for your seemingly petty purpose in the missing of meals. There is great power in the place of turning your natural appetites over to God. In fact, it is one of the ways His purposes are fulfilled.

This will be an insightful journey into what it looks like for your life to become a weapon in the hand of God. A weapon through strategically posturing your life in fasting and prayer to see His divine purposes fulfilled. It is sure to be a wild ride! This book will be about you giving your life over to Jesus in the secret place of fasting and prayer.

Much has already been written to create a proper foundation in my first book on fasting, *Fasting: Rediscovering the Ancient Pathways*, so we won't spend much time laying a foundation of that sort again. We will hop right into it. This is your day. Now is your time.

Oh joy-filled traveler of this ancient pathway of fasting and prayer, I pray that you hear the voice of the Bridegroom wooing your heart into deeper places of intimate experience in Him, for all of this is an issue and a matter of love.

God takes lovers and turns them into leaders; lovers always make better leaders. What confidence in God there is to know that you have been set free. Free from the strength of your own will and the demand to have it all your way. Free to be joyfully consumed with Jesus and to be immersed into the deep end of His delight for your life.

His love has raptured my heart and set my gaze upon things above. And from this place, I can now see what real purpose and the ultimate issues are in the earth. May He touch you and allow you to see. May He overwhelm you and free you from the captivity of the pressures of defining your life by the standards of the world. May He become all to you, and fill all of you afresh, so you can offer up to Him what it is that He desires most—all of you!

My friend, it is time to give it all to Him. Your attention, yes. Your affection, yes. But, also your appetite, yes! May your loving devotion unto Jesus in the place of fasting and prayer see lives changed, cities shaken, regions transformed, and nations redeemed. Beloved, let's fast and pray and let God use our lives as weapons in His mighty hand!

CHAPTER 1

SETTING THE STAGE

We live in a time where what the world is in need of is more broken people. We must not be mistaken. When I say that what the world is in need of is more broken people, I mean exactly that. The world needs people who have been broken by the love of God. The stage of the world has been set and God longs to plug people into His unfolding drama. The eyes of the Lord are searching throughout the earth, looking for a heart that is fully His on whose behalf He can show Himself strong.[4]

The Lord searches for people who long to have their life count. The eyes of the Lord canvas the earth in search of anyone whose heart burns to see their life

---

[4] 2 Chron 16:9, NLT

make a mark. If you have a jealousy that resides in you to see your life impact the world and change the course of history as we know it, the Lord is looking for you.

This longing is not to be overlooked. This burning within is not just to be cast off as some grave impossibility. No, no, no, please pay attention. Please be attentive to your heart in these matters, for God initiates and then waits to see who will respond to His tug.

When we mention a broken people we definitely are not thinking in worldly terms. The common ways that the world quickly and critically categorizes people as broken for a variety of self-concluded issues that each has determined to be wrong with another is not at all what the reference is here. However, there is a very real brokenness that the world doesn't quickly identify or isn't even willing to acknowledge. There are those who are broken and don't know it because the world has celebrated their condition for so long that it has fed what God has desired to starve.

In my early days of walking with the Lord I thought I wanted to be a great leader. I prayed hard and long for God to use my life in some incredible leadership capacity. I burned with a very real zeal for the Lord to raise me up and set me in a prominent leadership role that would influence my generation and change the world. I wanted my life to count. I wanted to see the world shaken, and I wanted God to use my life to do it. And over time it isn't that the cry from within me has changed drastically. In fact, for the most part it is still there and as fiery as ever.

The one thing that has changed without a doubt is that I no longer have a wild desire to be a great leader. At least that isn't what is at the forefront of my concern. I have realized over time with Him that I would rather be a great lover. Lovers always make better leaders, at least in a Kingdom sense they do. God will take great lovers and make them great leaders.

A seed will always reproduce its own kind. It's critically important that we esteem loving over leading. It is necessary to set them in the right order. For, you may find yourself leading for Him, and maybe even leading well, but it won't always guarantee that you will love Him, or love Him well for that matter. Loving Jesus is everything, and everything else that He wants to do must flow from there.

Loving Jesus is everything, and everything else that He wants to do must flow from there.

The world needs people that are totally wrecked by the love of God. The world needs people that are completely sold out to Jesus and His heart. A people that are broken and entered into His brokenness through the influence that His love has had on their hearts. A people that have willingly and joyfully abandoned the direct pursuit of the things of this world because all of their life and their desires are fulfilled and realized in Him.

A people who don't only sing and pray about this world not being their home, but who actually live like it. A people who don't only sing about giving their life away because it doesn't belong to them, but in the deep and real practical places of their hearts and lives have turned themselves over to Jesus for whatever He would say and wherever that would go.

The world needs lovers of Jesus who love Him for Him and don't manipulate their love of Him for the things that come from Him.

The world needs lovers of Jesus to surface. The world needs lovers of Jesus marked by purity and innocence. The world needs lovers of Jesus who love Him for Him and don't manipulate their love of Him for the things that come from Him. Oh, what a desperate day and time we find ourselves in, longing and crying out to God for such a people.

Where are those who have lost their desire for the world and its things because you have realized that everything you will ever need is found in Him? Where are those who are hungering and thirsting after righteousness because you have come to know that it is in this place where the promise of being filled lies? Where are those who are broken of the pursuit of riches because you understand He is the greatest treasure, the pearl of great price, the costliest of all the gems to be had?

Where are those who are no longer given over to chasing power, fame, influence, and the exaltation of their own name because you have come to realize that there is only One worthy to be exalted? There is one name that heaven shouts, and inasmuch as this may be a bubble-bursting revelation to you—it is not your name; it is not my name; it is the name of Jesus!

Where are those who have lost their desire for the world and its things because you have realized that everything you will ever need is found in Him?

Too many are given over to the vain pursuits that the world around us offers. Too many are caught up in the fanfare, the popularity, the stardom, and the lights, camera, action whirlwind that society has created. Too many have bought into the lie that seizing worldly attraction is synonymous with fulfilling God's purposes.

The world doesn't need more people that just want to be famous. The world doesn't need more people that just want to be rich. The world isn't waiting for another person to arise that wants to be socially accepted. The world doesn't need somebody else that has all of the political prowess and can sway crowds with ear-tickling articulation. The world isn't in need of another person who will bend under the demands of financial stature and be governed by the wealthy influence and investing of those around them.

The world is not hungering after another person who is chasing down the glitz, glamour, and applause of the world's hollow pursuits. **God is looking for a people that just want Jesus.** The world isn't waiting for the next somebody to make it big or arrive. In fact, the world has enough of these. And, as sad as it is to say, the Kingdom of God has enough of these. This definitely isn't what the world needs, and it for sure is not what God is searching for.

God is looking for a people who will love Jesus more than ministry. God is looking for a people who will love Jesus more than they love their donors. God is looking for a people who will love Jesus more than they love popularity. God is looking for a people who love Jesus more than they love their own gifting.

God is looking for a people who love Jesus more than they love certain social circles, relational networks, streams of ministry, open doors of invitations, and all that comes with this nonsensical web of entanglements. God is looking for a people that just want Jesus.

Are you willing to simply give all of your heart and its devotion to Jesus? Then God has something to work with. However, this isn't only the beginning place; it is the *only* place. Many begin broken and then over time become inflated by their own idea of themselves. Many begin humbled before the Lord and then morph into something else when all of the unique pressures, influences, and strategic weapons of warfare hit their hearts.

Brokenness is not just the key that opens the door. Brokenness is the key and the motor oil that continually fuels all of our endeavors with the Lord. Brokenness will either empower us or become us. We will either continually cling to Jesus and love Him above all things or be broken by the weight of the other corruptions that become us over time as we take our gaze off of the One who mattered most in the beginning.

> **Brokenness is the key and the motor oil that continually fuels all of our endeavors with the Lord.**

Man has a plethora of methods, but God has a prescription. God's prescription for those who will inherit the earth is brokenness. Matthew tells us that blessed are the meek, for they shall inherit the earth.[5]

---

[5] Matt 5:5, NKJV

This is a formula that man has attempted to dodge—the meek, lowly, broken pathway into and unto being conformed to the image of Jesus.

The prideful self-exaltation of the fleshly nature is radically opposed to the idea of lowering oneself. The demand the flesh places upon our lives for independence from God and His ways is a violent tug-of-war in and within the heart. Rather than fully yielding to the prescription that God has made, man has found a variety of ways into the same outcome that God has promised. Because this is a promise, the meek will inherit the earth.

Meekness is not weakness. It is actually the exact opposite; it is strength that has been surrendered.

We must understand that meekness is not weakness. It is actually the exact opposite; it is strength that has been surrendered. God's power source is meekness, lowliness, and brokenness. The One who has all power and carries all authority is simultaneously the Lamb that was slain. The One who is worthy to open the scroll is the same One that took on the form of a servant and emptied Himself unto death.

God's own chosen method to change the world was through the laying down of His own life, in lowliness, in brokenness. And so it is with those that He uses to change the world now. It is unto the broken, unto the meek, that God chooses to allow to inherit the earth and wield His authority. As I heard it so well put, "The meek shall inherit and rule the earth because the meek One rules the heavens."[6] It is important that we don't fight God's way, but rather identify it and yield to the work of the Holy Spirit within us to make us more like Him.

God wants to use your life to change the world. It is necessary to note that there are many that have ventured off into this direction with eyes blazing and hearts stirred only to realize the cost of such a request. Jesus said it best when He was speaking to the disciples with Him. He said, "For whoever wishes to save his life will lose it; but whoever loses his life for My sake will find it. For what will it profit a man if he gains the whole world and forfeits his soul? Or what will a man give in exchange for his soul?"[7]

I would find it best at this point to say that God is not simply looking for those who may feel they have the right tools or willpower in order for Him to use them, no. God is looking for a people who are willing to enter into His brokenness, to share in the fellowship of His sufferings, to be made by Him what they could never make themselves. Not just in the exterior façade and imagery, but deep within, the substance

---

[6] David Popovici, Jesus 19 Conference, Orlando, FL, 2019.
[7] Matt 16:25-26, NASB

and stature that can only be forged by the work of the Spirit.

Jesus said that those who spend their time trying to protect and keep will ultimately end up losing. But for those of us who choose to lose all things unto Him and for Him, we will end up finding what we have always been looking for.

For those of us who choose to lose all things unto Him and for Him, we will end up finding what we have always been looking for.

God is more interested in your brokenness than your giftedness. Yes, you read that correctly. He can impart giftedness in a moment, for the Spirit distributes gifts to each one just as He wills.[8] That's the easier part for the Lord. But brokenness is something that must be entered into. You can teach and impart gifting, but brokenness requires a response of the heart.

Many begin broken, but somewhere along the way end up feeling very capable. Remember Saul, hiding in the beginning, and then after you turn a few pages he has a massive monument for himself that is to be adored.[9] What a shame it is, yet how quickly it happens. Brokenness must be guarded; it must be cherished. For

[8] 1 Cor 12:11, NASB
[9] 1 Sam 15:12, CSB

herein lies the beauty of God's authority—He is Lion and Lamb.

Fasting is a gift in our lives to self-perpetuate the beauty of brokenness. At one point it is the psalmist who declares, "I humbled my soul with fasting..."[10] Hear those words: I humbled my soul. This is by deliberate decision. These are the words of one who has calculated the cost and yet also determined the reward.

Fasting is a gift in our lives to self-perpetuate the beauty of brokenness.

May your love for Him help to lead countless others throughout the earth into this place of self-abandoned devotion. Let them call you wild. Let them call you radical. Let them criticize and categorize; it's okay. You are not living for a momentary opinion. You are not living for applause in the earth. You are not given over to the catering and preferring mentalities that are jockeying for position. You belong to Him and this world is not your home.

---

[10] Ps 35:13, NASB

CHAPTER 2

MYSTERY AND SECRETS

Mystery

1. Anything that is kept secret or remains unexplainable or unknown.
2. Any affair, thing, or person that presents features or qualities so obscure as to arouse curiosity or speculation.
3. Any truth that is unknowable except by divine revelation.[11]

Our God is full of mystery. He is not just full of mystery, as if to assume that mystery was something He has learned along the way of His existence,

---

[11] Dictionary.com., https://www.dictionary.com/browse/mystery?s=t

but mystery is His makeup; our God is mysterious. Our God is distinctly marked by and has chosen to be revealed and known through mystery. There is much about Him that is mysterious.

For example, the reality of the Trinity. He is one, yet has chosen to reveal Himself in three distinct persons: Father, Son, and Spirit. He is revealed as three, yet these three are all one and know a unity unlike anything the earth has seen or knows in comparison to use as a reference point for explanation.

The expression of their being three does not sever the harmony they know as one. They are not in competition with one another. They lovingly and joyfully prefer and serve one another. The Trinity is a mystery. The Trinity is beyond the scope of man's intellectual might. There are many things about our God that are this way, simply and profoundly mysterious.

Bound up within Him are the riches of secrets and mysteries. They are not bound up within Him like some secret vault with an impenetrable exterior, or even a safe with an unknown code. In fact, it is quite different than that. David reveals to us and brings encouragement to us that He is a covenant-keeping God that reserves certain secrets for those covenant lovers that fear Him.[12]

---

[12] Ps 25:14, NASB

God has allowed it to be this way. He prefers this place of mystery. He has hemmed Himself up into wonder and awe. He reserves much to be known about Himself for those who come honestly seeking, hungry, and with their whole heart. Jeremiah, out of God's desire to be known, prophesies and writes, "You shall seek Me and find Me when you search for Me with all of your heart."[13]

Praise God for this glorious pursuit of mystery. For it is not some unmanageable game of hide-and-seek that we are a part of. He is not hiding Himself in mystery because He has no desire to be found. He longs to be found. The whole point is for hungry seekers to find Him. He jealously waits to be sought after. To these, He has chosen to unreservedly reveal Himself.

God doesn't limit Himself to the natural mind and its attempt to find Him and define Him. Our God places Himself right outside the boundaries of what we might consider to be reason or natural sense. For much about Him doesn't fit well into the natural mind's attempt to make sense of Him.

The greatest of philosophers and the most premier thinkers the world has ever known fall short in their attempt to box God into the capacity of their thinking

---

[13] Jer 29:13, NASB

and research. For God has created the human mind and then determined that He will not be limited by it. With all of man's attempts to find God and define Him, there is a truth that remains, and it is this—there is much to know about God that simply cannot be researched; it must be revealed.

Research is wonderful and it holds an important place in life for a variety of things, but God chooses to process Himself into the heart and life of His sons and daughters, not by way of research, but by way of revelation; He longs to reveal Himself. God has made it this way. It is not to the high and mighty that He chooses to give of Himself, but unto the childlike.

It is not to the high and mighty that He chooses to give of Himself, but unto the childlike.

With a heart filled with childlikeness there are some important places throughout the Scriptures that provide for us a glimpse into the wisdom that God establishes through mystery. Paul in his first letter to the church at Corinth wrote these words, "A person should think of us in this way: as servants of Christ and managers of the mysteries of God."[14]

---

[14] 1 Cor 4:1, CSB

Paul's exhortation is that when people consider our lives, there is something that should be a part of the conclusion they come to. It is the fact that we are not subject to our own fleshly wisdom, but that our God, who is filled with mysteries and secrets, chooses to share those with His people, and we are now managers of those secrets.

Another word for manager is steward, which means to faithfully oversee something that has been placed within our care or oversight. Our lives should be lived in a way that is deemed to be faithful with the mysteries God has revealed to us.

Our lives should be lived in a way that is deemed to be faithful with the mysteries God has revealed to us.

Paul's charge to the believers in Corinth needs to be heard and applied in a fresh way to our hearts and lives today. The mysteries that God longs to reveal, and has revealed, await the stewardship of faithful lovers.

When people see and interact with your life there should be a sense that your life is not governed by the same fleshly limitations that the rest of the world is subjected to. For the world has its wisdom, and it is fitting and applauded by many for a variety of reasons. But our lives have been filled with a wisdom that doesn't have its origin in this world. Our lives have been infused with a wisdom that is from above.

James, in referencing the differences in wisdoms, says that there is a wisdom that is earthly, unspiritual, and demonic. He also then tells of another kind of wisdom, a wisdom that is from above.[15] Our hearts have been opened to the wisdom that is from above, the wisdom that bears God's heart and His ways.

As one filled with the Holy Spirit, God has now made it possible for you to not just know Him, but to know what is bound up within His heart and mind.

We are not limited to our fleshly capacities because we have been filled with the precious Holy Spirit. The Holy Spirit has broken off of our lives all of the excuses for us to be defined by a fleshly wisdom. You are not like everyone else in the world. As a lover of Jesus and one filled with His Spirit, your life has been marked by an otherworldly reality. You no longer fit nice and neat within the world.

You are now in the world, yet you are not of it.[16] As one filled with the Holy Spirit, God has now made it possible for you to not just know Him, but to know what is bound up within His heart and mind. Let

---

[15] James 3:15; 17, NASB
[16] John 17:15-16, NASB

us consider the following passage found in the letter written to the Corinthians by Paul,

"But as it is written: 'Eye has not seen, nor ear heard, nor have entered into the heart of man the things which God has prepared for those that love Him.' But God has revealed them to us through His Spirit. For the Spirit searches all things, yes, the deep things of God. For what man knows the things of a man except the spirit of the man which is in him? Even so no one knows the things of God except the Spirit of God. Now we have received, not the spirit of the world, but the Spirit who is from God, that we might know the things that have been freely given to us by God. These things we also speak, not in words which man's wisdom teaches but which the Holy Spirit teaches, comparing spiritual things with spiritual. But the natural man does not receive the things of the Spirit of God, for they are foolishness to him; nor can he know them, because they are spiritually discerned. But he who is spiritual judges all things, yet he himself is rightly judged by no one. For, 'who has known the mind of the

LORD that he may instruct Him? But we have the mind of Christ.' "[17]

The wisdom that is from above, revealed to us by the Spirit, is foolishness to the natural mind. The natural mind reacts in hostility to, and is radically objected to, the wisdom revealed to us by God's Spirit, and it is meant to be this way. For the natural mind is not the necessary container to bear that which God reveals.

The natural mind is not the necessary container to bear that which God reveals.

God has chosen to process Himself into the hearts and lives of those that love Him by way of revelation, and that revelation comes by way of His own Spirit, which now resides in us. It is God in us that helps us to know God Himself. He comes in us—we are filled with His Spirit—and then reveals Himself within us. It takes God to know God. It is God in you that is continually revealing God to you. Praise God!

It is now one of the roles of the Spirit within us to reveal to us the deep things of God. The Holy Spirit working within you constantly reveals and bears witness to God's wisdom that is being made known

---

[17] 1 Cor 2:9-16, NKJV

to you. Our lives are no longer simply captive to the tyranny of reason and sense; we have God's wisdom to rely upon.

God's wisdom will at times call us to do things that don't fit well within the realm of what makes the most sense. God's wisdom, when revealed by His Spirit, will sometimes place our lives into peculiar places. God doesn't seem to be most concerned with making sure that our lives are always aligned perfectly with how we at times determine what would make the most sense.

It is God in you that is continually revealing God to you.

If you have walked with Jesus for any amount of time, you know the truth of what I am saying and how it applies to our loving obedience to Him. Obedience, at times, becomes troublesome, because it calls us beyond the current boundaries of our ability to rationalize what would be best, or what we deem to be possible.

It is important to make note that at times this will be a fierce battle, because God's ways are not our ways and His thoughts are not our thoughts; His ways and His thoughts are higher than ours.[18] You will not be able to manage God's wisdom by fleshly mechanisms.

---

[18] Isa 55:8-9, NASB

What is revealed by the Spirit will require dependency upon the Spirit to see it through.

God has not enabled a combination of the two, the flesh and the Spirit. His desire is that what is born of the Spirit be carried out by His Spirit. There is a tendency within us, if we are not careful and aware of what is actually happening, to want to carry out things that have been revealed by the Spirit in a fleshly way that absolves us of dependency on God. God will have none of this. The Spirit doesn't only reveal the what, but also the way. We must remain discerning and dependent.

There are many throughout the history of the Scriptures that were placed in situations by way of obedience to God that didn't make any sense at all. If you have ever felt the tug upon your own heart to walk with God in a way that didn't fit all that well into the wisdom of other people's boxes, rest assured you are not alone. There have been many that have gone before you that don't fit well into the container that the natural mind and its wisdom has created an allowance for.

Abraham left all of the wealth and inheritance that he ever knew for a place that God would reveal, whose city and maker was God Himself.[19] Moses stood before

---

[19] Gen 12:1-5, NASB

a powerful Pharaoh and believed that the great I AM was with him to deliver a nation.[20] Gideon sifted down his army to three hundred in order to confront the enemy that was opposing them as a people.[21] Elijah stood on top of Mt. Carmel and waited for fire to come down out of heaven as he called upon the name of the Lord.[22]

Our hearts should burn to be faithful stewards of God's mysteries.

John the baptizer preached to the king in his time about the sinfulness of his behavior and lost his head for it.[23] Stephen stood faithfully against the gnashing of teeth and stones flung in his direction.[24] John the beloved faithfully loved Jesus after a believed attempt to boil him alive had failed and put him into exile on the isle of Patmos.[25]

These are just to name a few. If you feel invited into a place that doesn't quite add up when you calculate it by the world's wisdom and the ways that it appreciates and applauds, don't worry, beloved one. You're standing amongst a great host of faithful ones.

---

[20] Ex 5:1, NASB
[21] Judges 7:2-7, NASB
[22] 1 Kings 18:20-40, NASB
[23] Matt 14:1-12, NASB
[24] Acts 7:54-60, NASB
[25] Rev 1:9, NASB

Our hearts should burn to be faithful stewards of God's mysteries. It is God's desire that His wisdom will be embedded in our lives and that it will affect everything about us. How we set up our lives should be in light of these mysteries, these secrets that God has revealed, and longs to reveal. Here are some other places throughout Scripture where we can create a reference point for secrets and mystery in order to find great encouragement:

"It is the glory of God to conceal a matter, but the glory of kings is to search out a matter."[26]

"May the name of God be praised forever and ever, for wisdom and power belong to him. He changes the times and seasons; he removes kings and establishes kings. He gives wisdom to the wise and knowledge to those who have understanding. He reveals deep and hidden things; he knows what is in the darkness, and light dwells with him."[27]

---

[26] Prov 25:2, NKJV
[27] Dan 2:20-22, CSB

"The secret counsel of the LORD is for those who fear him, and he reveals his covenant to them."[28]

"He reveals mysteries from the darkness and brings the deepest darkness into the light."[29]

It is now with this framework for secrets and mystery that we have created that we consider how this directly affects the place of fasting and prayer. Fasting is a mystery. Fasting is mysterious, for within the means of something so foolish and weak God has chosen to reveal His wisdom and strength. Fasting is foolishness to the natural mind. Well, it is important to note that fasting as consecration and a devotional expression of hunger unto Jesus is foolishness to the natural man.

Fasting is mysterious, for within the means of something so foolish and weak God has chosen to reveal His wisdom and strength.

In our day fasting has been applauded and incorporated into people's lifestyles for a variety of reasons: intermittent fasting for health and physique; liquid and water fasting for medical purposes and surgical

---

[28] Ps 25:14, CSB
[29] Job 12:22, CSB

procedures; fasting by other religious expressions with a variety of motivations attached to it; other styles of fasting as a means to arrive at certain conclusions that have been deemed as okay or necessary according to the natural man and its ways. The natural man has a place and a purpose for fasting, just not as an expression of hunger and a longing to be filled with the life of God in a greater way.

As a lover of Jesus, we cannot afford to miss God's wisdom found in the place of fasting.

Even against all of the objections that can be thrown up to the practice of fasting, we come lovingly to the face of God found in the person of Jesus and His wisdom granted to us by His own Spirit. As a lover of Jesus, we cannot afford to miss God's wisdom found in the place of fasting. Deeply woven into the life of a covenant lover of Jesus is God's desire for fasting. It is His own wisdom. It is His own selection and preference. Unto those who choose to yield to Him and His desires, according to Jesus, we are to be found fasting.[30]

A heart posture of childlikeness is required in the place of fasting. It cannot be approached with all of the craftiness of human wisdom, for the gems to be had will never be mined this way. Right in the middle

---

[30] Matt 9:15, NKJV

of something so offensive, something so simple, something so outrightly disgusting of an idea to our flesh and its will, is the beauty of fasting. Fasting must be a simple act of obedience to God. Any more of an attempt to analyze fasting will prove to be a breeding ground for frustration.

The natural mind is not meant to be perfectly compatible with the things God chooses to reveal by His Spirit. For it is in this simple act of obedience that God has chosen, by His own wisdom, to deposit and make possible powerful supernatural results. There is much that God does in the place of fasting, both in us and around us, that are simply because His wisdom has determined it to be this way.

Paul writes these words about God's wisdom, "Let no one deceive himself. If anyone among you thinks that he is wise in this age, let him become a fool that he may become wise. For the wisdom of this world is folly with God. For it is written, 'He catches the wise in their craftiness,' and again, 'The Lord knows the thoughts of the wise, that they are futile.' "[31]

The natural mind is not meant to be perfectly compatible with the things God chooses to reveal by His Spirit.

---

[31] 1 Cor 3:18-20, ESV

There must be a divine element to our obedience unto God in the place of fasting. Anything other than this would wrestle the mind out of its ability to yield in the place of fasting. You really and honestly have to choose to believe that there is a divine infusion in the place of fasting, that God is able to work within the place of our obedience unto Him to bring about His own desired conclusions through our denial of food or certain foods altogether, for whatever time period. Also, you honestly have to be a little out of your right mind according to the world to fully subject yourself to God in the place of fasting.

Fasting is weakness, yet weakness that bears God's strength. Fasting is foolishness, yet foolishness that bears God's wisdom.

With the analyzing of the right mind according to the world we consider that many others who make such decisions don't reap the same reward that we do out of the place of obedience. Take a Daniel Fast, for instance, with the simple removal of meat and sweets. A vegetarian isn't reaping the same reward as the one who chooses to yield to God for a season in this style of fast.

Have you ever taken a moment to think about something like this? It is totally wild! However, it is also true. So, what is it, then, about a fasted life that makes its potency so powerful and dynamic? It is God's own choosing to use it as a tool for Him to build and form His own desires.

We have become fools to the world so that we might be able to bear God's wisdom. We know and choose to believe that within the place of our yes to God in fasting He has reserved the right to work on our behalf for His own desires. In the simple and practical dietary modifications that we make out of our discerning of His loving invitation and wisdom we say yes to Him. In these simple dietary changes God works powerfully.

It sounds really foolish, right? To the natural mind it is an absolute affront. God chooses foolishness to confound the world's wisdom. God chooses weakness to bind up the world's strength. Fasting is weakness, yet weakness that bears God's strength. Fasting is foolishness, yet **Fasting isn't just about turning from food; it is equally and more powerfully about turning to Him.** foolishness that bears God's wisdom. God has allowed the offense of fasting to be one of the ways that He reserves it for those who simply have a heart filled with a yes to Him.

Do you have an unconditional yes to Him? Have you been offended by the invitation to fasting? God isn't going to change His own wisdom to accommodate your lack of desire. Lack of desire? Yes, fasting isn't just about turning from food; it is equally and more powerfully about turning to Him.

Many times, God will package exactly what we need the most and have been crying out for in a package that offends us. We miss it because we are offended by it. We are offended by the way that it comes to us. We are offended by the way that God has chosen to answer. We never search a matter out fully because of the offense of our flesh, natural mind, and way that we would prefer God to move and do things.

Many times, God will package exactly what we need the most in a package that offends us.

There are desires that God has which will be fulfilled through a people who get overtaken by His heart in fasting and prayer. Kingdoms shaken. Enemies defeated. Cities and regions turned upside down. The powerful advance of the Kingdom and the establishing of God's loving rule amongst the nations of the earth. A people of great violence who will arise, not with worldly weapons to engage their warfare, but with weapons that are divine in nature, even to the bringing down and demolishing of strongholds. People who have been apprehended by a love that has totally ruined them for any other one or any other thing; totally sold out for love's sake to the King of Kings and Lord of Lords and His chosen prescription to bring His Kingdom on earth as it is in heaven!

All of this and much more are upon the lives of the faithful ones given over in fasting and prayer. This is one of God's chosen methods. Fasting is a divine weapon. It is not up to us whether or not God will use this way. He has already determined it to be so. It is only up to us whether or not we will throw our lives into the way that God has already chosen.

CHAPTER 3

SHAKERS AND SHAPERS

"We have taught a generation to feast and play but the times demand that we fast and pray."[32]

—Lou Engle

In my first book on the subject of fasting, *Fasting: Rediscovering the Ancient Pathways,* we took much time to create a foundation that would allow a proper place for the conversation that we are initiating here. We completely pointed the lifestyle practice of fasting and prayer at someone, that person being Jesus, the Son of God.

Rightfully so, we didn't attempt to take the practical expression of turning our natural appetite over to

---

[32] Lou Engle, https://www.inspiringquotes.us/author/5598-lou-engle.

Jesus and turn that into a means to an end. The means is loving Jesus. The end is loving Jesus. Loving devotion to Jesus is what sustains it all along the way.

Loving Jesus, and learning to love Him well, will always be the greatest accomplishment in the place of fasting.

It is all about Jesus. So, this is not being mentioned to suggest that there is now something greater, or something other, to talk about that needed that as a preface, not at all. Loving Jesus, and learning to love Him well, will always be the greatest accomplishment in the place of fasting.

Our self-denial in an intentional way, turning over the hunger of our natural man, awakens a burning love for the Son of God that is unparalleled to any other experience. God has selected the practice of fasting in the life of a lover of Jesus as a specialized tool to bring awakening and increased hunger for Him into our lives. Our denial of natural hunger awakens and increases our spiritual hunger. The denial of natural bread is a catalyst of sorts to ignite the fuse of hunger for Him who is the bread of life.

Fasting is always to be pointed at someone—that person being forever and always Jesus. However, as we search the Scriptures it is undeniable that God uses fasting to fulfill certain purposes that are in His heart. We could say it this way. We point our fasting at someone—Jesus—and God will at times point our fasting at something.

As we read through the Scriptures, we have many examples of men and women that God gripped in the place of fasting and prayer that seemed to posture themselves in a unique way for God to do incredible things. There is an obedience that echoes throughout the Bible in the lives of men and women that God called to fast and then used their obedience in fasting as a weapon of sorts to shake and shape history as we know it.

The lives of these men and women must not just be used as an illustrated message. The lives of these obedient ones that have gone before us cannot be left in the container of illustrations; rather, they must be freed to be seen through the lens of invitations. The stories we find are meant to do more

Our denial of natural hunger awakens and increases our spiritual hunger.

than inform us, although they do that very well. They are meant to also invite us. The stories inform us of the way that God speaks to and uses specific people that are sensitive to His voice.

Throughout the history found in the Bible there are many who were found fasting with a desire to be obedient in their day. But these same stories must not only inform us and leave us afar off in awe of how God chose to do those things with others, completely leaving our lives out of the equation of God using our lives in similar fashion. We must be informed and invited. We must receive a fresh invitation in our hearts and lives to take up the same place of loving obedience to see God use our lives as weapons in His hand to shake and shape history in *our* day!

He is counting on you to be awakened by His Spirit and to get involved in what He is doing.

There have been significant moments throughout history when the hearts of men and women have been gripped by God to recognize that a door of opportunity in the Spirit had been swung open. These precious and jealous ones determined to seize the moment by giving themselves in fasting and praying to contend and cry out for breakthrough, awakening, revival, and a powerful outpouring of God's Spirit.

Much of history is shaped by those who discern the day and seize the moment. It takes an active involvement, a participation with God for His desires to be fully realized in the earth. God has chosen to partner with His people. He will not compromise His own design. Therefore, He is counting on you to be awakened by His Spirit and to get involved in what He is doing.

One of the beautiful things about God is that He has empowered you to be able to make a choice. We would call this free will. God has placed within His creation the ability to make a choice, whether good or bad; you have the ability to make your own choice. This is one of the ways that God reveals His nature in being all-powerful. He doesn't create you and then just program you to have to do what He wants. He doesn't breathe life into you, and then force-fully puppeteer you to bid His wishes or perform His will. It is not like this at all.

Surrender must be out of love or else it isn't really real.

He is a loving God. He is a God that is completely secure in Himself. He is a God that trusts so greatly in His power and His influence in your heart and in your life that He doesn't have to do any of those weird things to force you to do anything; He loves you into surrender. He is confident that His loving influence in your heart and life over time will bring you to the place where He doesn't have to take anything from you, but where you will willingly and joyfully give Him all things.

Surrender must be out of love or else it isn't really real. It is God's great love for you that has brought you to the place where you are willing to lay your life down. Laying your life down is an act of love. Denying yourself of all of what you participate in or partake of must be continually fueled by an experience of a greater satisfaction than what is perceived to be missed out on. This is the great love of God that has come crashing into our hearts. It satisfies to the deepest depths and farthest corners.

Earthly and temporary satisfactions are completely engulfed into the supreme source of satisfaction, which is Christ Himself.

His love, alive and active within us, is what empowers us to be able to suffer the loss of things that others might not deem possible to go without. Because we have come alive in Him and love Him, our felt love and need for other things begins to diminish. Because we have Him, we don't need much else anymore. We have forsaken all things. Earthly and temporary satisfactions are completely engulfed into the supreme source of satisfaction, which is Christ Himself.

Because we have been loved well, we are willing to suffer well, with, and in Him. Suffer? Wait a minute… who's talking about suffering? Love includes suffering. Love includes many things, but suffering is definitely one of the ingredients. No man took Jesus' life from

Him; He laid it down on His own accord, and it was because of His incredible love for you.[33]

Because of Jesus' great love for you, and the joy set before Him, He suffered the scorn of the cross and endured its shame.[34] Love empowers suffering. It is the words of Paul that we are to be reminded of, "that I may know Him and the power of His resurrection and the fellowship of His sufferings, being conformed to His death."[35]

If you want to change the world you have to be willing to suffer. You aren't going to be able to be the same as everyone else. You aren't going to be able to live casually. You aren't going to be able to avoid the hard things, or the cost. If you want to shake your generation, you have to be willing to do what very few others are willing to do.

Changing the world has never happened accidentally. No one ever stumbled upon greatness or significance and was then clueless as to how they arrived there, at least not in God. If you want to shape history you have to consider the cost of love and be willing to go all in with God and suffer the consequences in living in a way that becomes common to you, though

---

[33] John 10:18, NASB
[34] Heb 12:2, NASB
[35] Phil 3:10, NASB

it is uncommon to many around you. Shaking your generation will come at a price.

There are individuals who have chosen the pathway of going all in with God throughout our history and have seen God do extraordinary things. God is searching for a heart that is fully His. We tend to read over that so quickly that we miss the little word in that sentence that makes

God is searching for a heart that is fully His.

all the difference—fully. A heart that isn't wavering because of its attraction to the world. A heart that isn't bound by the prideful and lustful desires of its own wants. A heart that has been completely given over—fully. God raises up consecrated lovers.

There is a verse in Matthew chapter 22 that has always stood out to me. For most of us, we will know it as it reads this way, "For many are called, but few are chosen."[36] The reading of this verse at face value makes a few things unclear. Who are the many? Why isn't it all? How does someone get chosen? What if I get called and then don't get chosen?

It is easy to come to all of these potential questions after reading this verse. However, that is until I came across this verse in The Passion Translation. I absolutely have fallen in love with the way that this verse

---

[36] Matt 22:14, ESV

reads in The Passion Translation. This is what it says, "For everyone is invited to enter in, but few respond in excellence."[37] This is a game changer!

In reading the verse in the previous version it didn't create any real way for me to be accountable. It created a situation where I am to understand that many are called. Okay. Got that part. Then, out of those many there will be a selection process that ensues, and only a few will actually be chosen from those who were initially invited. Got it. The only problem is that it doesn't really seem like a scenario where I have anything to do to be accountable in the midst of the selection process. At least, that's what I thought until I came across the verse in The Passion Translation.

We have to understand that everyone is invited. God has a wide-open invitation, and all are welcome to come running. However, though all may be invited, few are actually going to respond in excellence. The sad truth is that few are actually going to answer the call and give God an excellent yes. This is an individual yes. This is something that is between you and God. It matters that we mention it this way.

This is not some corporate, or group, response. When the crowd dwindles; when the support group fades; when the cheerleaders are gone, and the pep

---

[37] Matt 22:14, TPT

rally has long been over; this is a matter that is between you and God. All of those other things are wonderful and can help to serve certain purposes in different moments and seasons, but ultimately the issue is, how will you respond to the call of God that is on your life?

Are you willing to say yes? Are you willing to give Him the excellent yes that He is looking for? There is a price to pay to answer the call. There is a suffering to bear. Will you say yes to the call if it costs you some friends? Will you say yes if it costs you a job? Will you say yes if it costs you a certain lifestyle or financial status? Will you say yes if you have to say it all by yourself? Even if no one else goes with you or says yes to the Lord the way that you are, will you say yes?

This is the issue, and one that many have confronted and determined that the price to move forward with God in certain ways was just more than they were willing to bear. As heartbreaking as it may sound, it is true.

In our attempt to give an excellent yes to God and His desires for us, we must look at Jesus. Jesus has made a way for us. Jesus was and is God and was a man that was filled with God. In our conversation of paying the price, even if alone and surrendering our lives to God in an excellent way, it must always lovingly bring us back to the person of Jesus.

A man tempted on every side and every way yet was without sin.[38] A man who had to have His face-off with isolation in the wilderness of fasting, a face-to-face confrontation with the devil himself, and a barrage of opportunities that the enemy provided to compromise God's design in His life.

When considering our own life, we must always look to the life of Jesus.

When considering our own life, we must always look to the life of Jesus.

At the waters of baptism at the Jordan River, Jesus has the dove rest upon Him and the voice of the Father thunder over Him. Immediately following this wild experience in His life, the Bible says the Holy Spirit thrusts Him into the wilderness where He fasted for forty days and was tempted by the enemy.[39]

In the wilderness, on an empty stomach of fasting, Jesus does what Adam couldn't do in the garden on a full stomach. In the wilderness, Jesus allowed the power of God's Word to work for Him in His confrontation against the enemy and his attempts, which is what the children of Israel were not able to do. In the isolation, in the wilderness surroundings, in the painful surrender to God of forty days, Jesus overcame. Jesus overcame the temptation to bow out of God's way.

---

[38] Heb 4:15, NASB
[39] Luke 4:1-2, NASB

After fasting for forty days and overcoming all of the temptations of His own flesh and the weapons of warfare that the enemy strategically formed against Him, Jesus arises out of the wilderness full of the power of the Holy Spirit! He goes in full of the Holy Spirit and comes out after fasting, crushes His own fleshly persuasions, and defeats the enemy, full of the power of the Holy Spirit.

He immediately preaches the Kingdom, heals the sick, casts out devils, and raises the dead. His victory in the wilderness was the hinge that unleashed a dynamic expression of Kingdom power and fruitfulness in life. Gaining authority over His own flesh and the manipulative attempts of the enemy in His life empowered Jesus to flow freely and fully in the manifestation of His Father's desires for Him. There was no blockage. There was no resistance. Everything had been confronted and defeated.

There is something about defeating our flesh and the enemy's influence in our heart and life that allows us to rise up in power.

There is something about the wilderness with God and forty days of fasting. Could it be that the wilderness of fasting in your life is what God is drawing you into to defeat the persuasions that your flesh has always used to convince you out of God's purposes for your life? Could it be that the wilderness of fasting is what God is longing to pull you into to confront and conquer the voice of the enemy in your life? Could it be that the wilderness of fasting is what God is intending to use in your heart and life to reveal the areas where your flesh or the enemy have led you into entertaining the compromising of God's way, His design, for your life?

We look at Jesus so that we can be mobilized unto and into God's purpose for our own lives.

Jesus is our example. There is something about defeating our flesh and the enemy's influence in our heart and life that allows us to rise up in power. It isn't that power is not always available for those that are filled with the Holy Spirit. Jesus went in filled with the Holy Spirit. But the dynamic expression of power that God desires becomes unrestricted when we deal with the issues in our own hearts that have a tendency to create hurdles and blockage. The problem is not on God's side, or with His desires for us.

Jesus is a beautiful example of a man that loved God with all of His heart, was sensitive to His voice and His desires in His life, and fully recognized the moment of opportunity that had been opened up to Him. Jesus discerned His day and fully seized the moment. Will you? We don't look at Jesus so that we can be paralyzed in awe. We look at Jesus so that we can be mobilized unto and into God's purpose for our own lives.

Jesus said, "Whoever believes in Me will also do the works that I do; and greater works than these will he do, because I am going to the Father."[40] Jesus is a wonderful example and a powerful invitation to great works in God.

God raises up people who have improbable beginnings and brings them into impossible outcomes.

We also have examples throughout the Bible that bear witness to the reality that God uses the lives of consecrated lovers to shake and shape history. God raises up people who have improbable beginnings and brings them into impossible outcomes. We will take a look at the lives of some of these powerful moments that we have to further expound on our point here and also provoke our hearts into a place of burning jealousy for God to take our lives and use them in like manner, to shake our generation and shape history!

There is much to be known about the lives of Moses, Esther, Daniel, Ezra, Jonah, Joel, and John the Baptist. However, for the point we are making, I would encourage you to read their lives more thoroughly than

---

40 John 14:12, ESV

what will be provided here. The next two chapters are not a biography about each one, but rather a specific pulling on and out of their lives in order to pull our lives into loving obedience to Jesus.

CHAPTER 4

MISSIONARIES AND DELIVERERS

Moses

There is much that can be said of the life of Moses. Moses is born during very hard and challenging days. The children of Israel are in the heat of the Egyptian captivity and have been living as slaves for quite some time. Moses survives the decree of the Pharaoh that all baby boys born to the Hebrews are supposed to be thrown into the river and killed. His mother sees that he is a beautiful child and chooses to hide him for three months.[41] He is later found by the

---

[41] Ex 2:2, NASB

daughter of Pharaoh and ends growing up in Pharaoh's own house.

It is years later when Moses is out one day and sees the hardship that the Israelites are enduring under the Egyptians. He witnesses an Egyptian beating an Israelite and decides to intervene in the situation and kill him. When Pharaoh heard about what happened he attempted to kill Moses, but he fled to Midian. This would be the beginning of a very long season of Moses' life, in the wilderness, being broken by God.

When God comes looking for Moses, he doesn't have an ounce of confidence in his ability to do what he feels God is asking of him.

I am sure we can all identify to some degree with where Moses is and what he is feeling. He is raised with a sense of his purpose in God; he feels a strong pull on his life toward being a deliverer for his people. The only problem is that, though he knows what he feels, he doesn't know how God wants him to walk that out. He carries ability and great zeal; he just hasn't yet learned to carry out what he feels he carries God's way. It is much later in Moses' life when he has the encounter with the burning bush.

God waits until Moses is completely broken. When God comes looking for Moses, he doesn't have an ounce of confidence in his ability to do what he feels God is asking of him. He isn't the younger, stronger, more determined version of himself anymore. Now he is older, somewhat weakened because of time and God's process, but most importantly he is a broken man. He has been broken of his desire to carry out God's plans his own way. It is going to have to be a miracle for God to be able to work with Moses, and thank God that this is exactly the place that He waited for Moses to come to so that He could do exactly that—work miracles with him.

Moses goes into Egypt with the Great I AM with him. He goes through a wild series of events with Pharaoh before he is willing to release the children of Israel. It is some time after the confrontation with Pharaoh, the miraculous exodus, crossing of the Red Sea, and destruction of Pharaoh and his army where we find the moment that I would like to highlight out of Moses' life.

Moses has already been through so much. But, the much that he has been through has created a unique capacity within him to desire God's voice and ways above his own abilities. Moses is now out in the wilderness journeying with the children of Israel towards the promise that God has given to them. Out here, again in the wilderness, Moses finds another invitation from God.

In Exodus chapter 24 we find Moses answering the call of God to go up the mountain and meet with Him there. God defined a specific place that He invited Moses to come and be with Him. We know from reading the story that when Moses reached the top of the mountain the cloud descended and the voice of God spoke to Moses out of the cloud and invited him in.

It just seems to be God's way. When He wants the whole, He targets the one.

Moses went into the cloud and spent forty days and forty nights in fasting and prayer, there with God, completely wrapped up and overwhelmed in the place of encounter.[42] It is in this account given for Moses' life that we find God using his act of obedience in fasting to provide significant and powerful breakthrough, not just for the life of Moses alone, but for an entire nation of people.

The children of Israel benefitted profoundly through the surrender of one man who chose to obey God. Interesting to consider that God will at times use the yes and life of one man to bring breakthrough to an entire nation. It just seems to be God's way. When He wants the whole, He targets the one. We see this pattern over and over again throughout the Scriptures.

---

[42] Ex 24:18, NASB

Abraham will be the father of many nations, but that is directly dependent upon how he stewards the life of one son being surrendered in his heart to God. Elijah is going to raise a dead nation back to life in God, but he is first tested with the life of a dead boy in an upper room. God Himself wants to redeem and reconcile all of the hostile nations of the earth back to Himself, so the way He chooses to reach all of the nations is by His selection of one nation, that being Israel. The pattern goes on and on. It is God's way.

When we see clearly and understand the pattern that God uses, we will not dismiss the powerful potential that our individual yes has to the Lord. God has, can, and will continue to use those who bring Him their yes to change the world. In fact, He takes great delight in overcoming the perceived insurmountable odds.

God has, can, and will continue to use those who bring Him their yes to change the world.

He joyously wows time and time again, as He is continually perceived as the underdog in all of the impossible scenarios that we find ourselves in, to bring impossibilities to their knees; to bring miracles out of messes; to create testimonies out of great tests. This is our God! You and God are the majority and the favorite in each and every situation that you may find yourself in. Now, back to Moses.

Moses finds himself in a forty-day and forty-night moment of obedience on top of the mountain with God. I am sure that like most of us he didn't have an idea that God was using his obedience as an offering that would shape history. This is a beautiful truth to consider. Most of us don't really know that our lives are being used to change the world when God calls us into moments of obedience, at times that are private in nature.

You and God are the majority and the favorite in each and every situation that you may find yourself in.

Moses is just responding to God the best way that he knows how to do. I absolutely love that! No professionalism. No other perks or incentives being offered to him. Just simple and wholehearted devotion to God. But he finds himself there atop the mountain in an intense encounter. It is during this encounter that God reveals to him His desires for the children of Israel. Moses receives the stone tablets that had the Law written upon them.

We have to understand the magnitude of the moment that Moses is experiencing. The Law revealed the desires of God to His people. The Law was the covenant offering from God to betroth Himself to Israel. The Law was the expression of God's desire to walk in covenant love and devotion with His people that He chose for Himself.

God freed them as a nation from Egypt out of slavery and bondage because of His great love for them and faithfulness to them. He freed them so that He might bring them to Himself. The Law could be seen as the marriage vows.

The Law was also strategic in that it became the tool for redemption for the other hostile pagan nations that surrounded Israel. God told them that if they would abide by the terms of the Law, He would make them a light. This light that God would make them would burn and shine brightly, thus providing a light tower in them as a people to bring hope and redemption to the other nations of the earth.

That ultimately didn't happen in the way that God desired, but that isn't the point of emphasis at this moment. You could think about it this way. The Law helped to mobilize Moses and the children of Israel for missions. It gave them a blueprint for life that would be missional.

God's love offering was the offering of the Law. The Law provided the necessary boundaries for God to be able to love them as a people the way He had always desired to. The Law was also the prescription to bring healing and wholeness from the broken attempts of their hearts and lives to intermingle and be influenced by the surrounding nations.

The hope-filled desire to bring redemption to the other nations and people groups surrounding Israel as a people was found in the Law. Wrapped up in the commandments as we know it was much more than cold and calloused behavioral modification requirements. The Law was filled with love and hope.

Moses' encounter provided breakthrough, deliverance, and hope for an entire nation. Moses' obedience to God in the place of fasting proved to be what God used to deliver all of His desires into the life of Moses, yes, but also the children of Israel as a whole. One man's yes brought breakthrough to a nation.

God used Moses' obedience as a gateway to get wisdom and counsel to a nation. God used Moses' surrender and consecration to provide a strategy for breakthrough that would deal with the ideals and practices of the surrounding pagan nations and their idol-worshiping cultures. God used Moses' life to provide revelatory insights to a nation on how to position themselves in the earth to fulfill His desires. This cannot be seen as some small issue. This is a massive ordeal.

God used Moses' surrender in an extraordinary way. And I know that may sound great as we consider the life of Moses, but I believe God wants to use the life of Moses to provoke you in a great way. What if your life and your personal and private devotion to God in fasting and prayer is what God is waiting to use to shape history? What if you have been dodging the very thing—that being fasting and praying—that God has chosen to use in your life and has been waiting for you to surrender to in order to shake the world and shape history?

The wilderness of fasting and prayer can help you to decrease so that He will increase.

Maybe you feel like Moses. You have had a sense of what God has put upon your life, but you just haven't yet been able to identify the way that you are to walk that out. Maybe you've tried to go for it and have fallen flat because you realize it was just your own effort attempting to wield something that you believed God has placed upon you or in your hands. It's okay. You too, like Moses, can experience the humbling and breaking in the wilderness.

Being broken by God is not a negative; it is actually a great positive. The wilderness of fasting and prayer can help you to decrease so that He will increase. The wilderness of fasting and praying can align you with the burning-bush moment of your life so that you too can receive divine instructions how to carry out all God equipped you to carry.

Even if you are one that considers yourself to be older in age, don't allow that to sway you from your purpose in God. Sometimes it takes the time that you thought was wasted in order to prepare you to enter into the greatest season of significance in your entire life.

God can speak to your heart and call you up the mountain to be with Him in fasting and prayer.

God can use your life of consecration as a means to bring breakthrough to an entire nation. As we look upon the life of Moses, God can speak to your heart and call you up the mountain to be with Him in fasting and prayer. There He can speak to you in a way that will bring strategic influence to nations and breakthrough to others. God can release His wisdom into your heart through fasting, fresh strategies, and blueprints for mobilization in missions.

We must allow Moses' life to crush the limitations we have placed and embraced upon our own singular yes to God. God can use one yes to change the world. He did it with Moses, and He can and desires to do it with you, but do you?

Esther

Esther is alive at a peculiar time in history. It is necessary that we set up a context for Esther's life so that the significance of her opportunity can be fully appreciated. The king, known by many as Xerxes, is ruling over 127 provinces through the region of Persia. His kingdom extends from India to Ethiopia. He is a man of great power and influence. The story of Esther opens with a banquet. On the seventh day of this banquet, King Xerxes summons the queen, Vashti, to come and appear before him so he can display her beauty before the people. Queen Vashti, who is hosting women at a separate banquet within the palace, refuses the call.

Xerxes becomes outraged and decides that the queen's disobedience cannot go unpunished. Vashti's act could potentially cause trouble in many ways for the rest of the men of the kingdom as other women might follow in the example of Vashti and disrespectfully be disobedient to their husbands. Xerxes follows the council of his advisors and bans Queen Vashti from his presence and palace, thus creating an opening for the position of queen in the kingdom.

Sometime later, after all of these things took place and King Xerxes' anger had subsided, he began to look for another queen. His council members suggested that he search throughout the provinces of his kingdom for every beautiful young virgin and allow one of them to replace the queen that had been banished. King Xerxes agrees to the plan and the search begins. This is where Esther enters our story.

Esther's parents have died. She is an orphan being raised by a relative, Mordecai. Esther and Mordecai are cousins. The Bible describes Esther as being beautiful in form and face.[43] Esther is one of the girls that is gathered by the search and brought to the palace for a period of preparation before she would go before the king. Once chosen, Mordecai instructs her not to reveal to anyone that she is a Jew, for the fear of how that might endanger her.

Esther undergoes one year of preparation to be presented before the king. This is in the hopes that in that one moment she would find the favor of the king and he might call her back by name into his presence.

The day finally comes where Esther has her opportunity. She goes before the king, in his presence. The king loves Esther more than all of the rest and the crown is placed on her head, thus making her the new queen, in the place of Vashti. This is where things get a little more interesting than they have already been.

After some time had passed, one day Mordecai was near the king's gate and overheard a plot by some of the king's officials to harm him. He shares this with Esther, and after an investigation, the men who had sought to

---

[43] Est 2:7, NASB

harm the king were hung on the gallows. After this, another man, Haman, is promoted into a high position to serve the king. All of the king's servants bowed down to Haman to pay homage, for King Xerxes had commanded this to be done.

Mordecai would not bow down to Haman, nor would he pay homage. Mordecai's refusal to bow down and pay homage to Haman became a serious issue and the king's servants questioned him as to his reason for transgressing the king's command. Mordecai revealed to them that he was a Jew.

Once the news was brought to Haman, he was furious. He decided that he would not only come after Mordecai, but that he would also destroy Mordecai and all of the people that he was a part of, thus putting a genocide notice on the Jewish people as a whole. Haman finagles his way through a conversation with the king and gets him to agree to sign off on the destruction of the Jewish people. Things have just gotten very serious.

The Bible tells us that as the notice went out throughout the provinces, great mourning hit the Jewish people. The Jews responded with weeping, wailing, and fasting. Many laid on sackcloth and ashes. The news would eventually reach the ears of Queen Esther in the palace, and great anguish came upon her at the thought of the destruction of her people.

Through a process of events and interactions, Mordecai sends a note to Queen Esther, pleading with her to go in before the king and implore him on behalf of the Jewish people. Queen Esther knows that no one is to go in before the king without being summoned. She understands that such behavior could potentially cost her her life.

In the heat of the moment Mordecai responds to Esther with words that help us to create a beautiful frame for God's desires here. Mordecai sends this exhortation to Esther, "Do not imagine that you in the king's palace can escape any more than all of the Jews. For if you remain silent at this time, relief and deliverance will arise for the Jews from another place and you and your father's house will perish. And who knows whether you have not attained royalty for such a time as this?"[44]

Let's take a moment to make sure that we are tracking together on what all is happening here. Esther is a Jew. She is an orphan girl, from a family that experienced exile all the way back under Nebuchadnezzar. She is being raised by her relative in the province of Susa under the rule of King Xerxes. She has been positioned in her province and processed into the palace where she is now the queen. She seems to carry a unique favor

---

[44] Est 4:13-14, NASB

on her life that has enabled her to triumph through a story filled with tragedy.

She is now prominent, though she comes from pitiful beginnings. Her platform in life carries great power, for she is the queen. She is the queen, but she is also a Jew, which no one yet knows, except for Mordecai. Her people are on the verge of experiencing one of the most treacherous acts ever known. Mordecai's exhortation comes to her, not as some quiet, pleasant request that could be ignored, but as a trumpeting that shakes her to her core.

It is in response to Mordecai's exhortation that we find the wisdom that Esther undertakes in the heat and hostility of the situation that she, and her people as a whole, are facing. Esther tells the messenger to reply to Mordecai with these words, "Go, assemble all the Jews who are found in Susa, and fast for me; do not eat or drink for three days, night or day. I and my maidens also will fast in the same way. And thus, I will go in to the king, which is not according to the law; and I if I perish, I perish."[45]

From this point we will shorten what is a much longer story. If you are familiar with the story, then you already understand that gallows had been constructed to hang Mordecai and it was the exact gallows that

---

[45] Est 4:16, NASB

Haman was hung on. The king found out about Haman's plotting and it cost him his life. Mordecai gets promoted, even to the degree of receiving the king's signet ring.

The king extended the golden scepter to Esther as she fell before the king on behalf of her people that the plan for the extinction would not be successfully carried out. All of the Jews are saved and they route their enemies throughout the provinces and land. The feast of Purim was instituted as a remembrance of the victory of the Lord they had all experienced.

God sees the needs of His people long before those needs even become reality.

Esther and Mordecai remain in power. In fact, Mordecai is last noted as the second most powerful man in the nation, second only to King Xerxes himself. This is an overwhelming story of trial and triumph, testing, and testimony.

From all there is to glean from the life and book of Esther, we will take the brief details we have shared thus far to illustrate a major point. God sees the needs of His people long before those needs even become reality. He providentially places those He can use in strategic places so they will be available when the crisis unfolds.[46]

---

[46] James E. Smith, *Old Testament Survey Series: The Books of History* (Joplin, MO: College Press Publishing Company, Inc., 2018), 41.

The story of Esther's life must be clearly seen and understood through God's desires to make a way for His people. God is the mastermind behind all of history as we know it, weaving and forming His desires through all of the complexities; many of which are outside of our immediate comprehension. God makes a way where there seems to be no way.

Esther's life, her position in the beginning, and process into the palace, was the way that God had formed her to be the answer in what was one of the darkest moments in the life and history of the Jewish people. Esther's life and her yes to God became an answer to her generation.

> **Esther's life and her yes to God became an answer to her generation.**

You may be wondering what fasting has to do with all of this. I am glad you asked. When Mordecai confronted Esther about the situation at hand, her response was to enter into a fast. Her people are on the verge of annihilation. There is a serious threat from the enemy in the works and about to come to fulfillment and Esther's battle strategy is to enter into a fast for three days without food or water. Seriously? Oh yes, seriously.

I am sure there were those waiting for Mordecai when he returned to hear the grand plan he and Esther had come up with that was going to allow them to prevail against the weapon the enemy had formed against them. I can almost imagine the looks on the faces of those that gathered with Mordecai when he was about to open up his mouth to release the wisdom that he and Esther felt God had given them to retaliate against the enemy and see the desires of God fulfilled for their people.

Can you see it? The eager anticipation because of the sobriety and intensity of the moment that they are all experiencing together? And then it happens, Mordecai shares the plan—we are not going to eat or drink for three days! What? Huh? Come again? No seriously, Mordecai. What's the plan that God will use to save us? What's the divine wisdom that you feel you've tapped into to save our people from the imminent attack and slaughter? And against all of the speculation and unbelief, Mordecai shares it again…we are going to fast!

You can almost see the utter disappointment on the faces of the people. Mordecai, we need a real strategy. Mordecai, surely there is something God has revealed to you for us to do that is actually going to be advantageous for us in the midst of such an extreme situation that we are facing. Mordecai, you cannot tell me that this is all.

Please understand. This is not to add to the biblical text. Rather, this is to consider their situation in light of our current experience and the lack of value as a whole that fasting receives. Fasting is foolishness; fasting is seen as weak. But also, embedded deep into the life of fasting, God has chosen to reveal His wisdom and strength. Even against all of the odds, they fasted, and they prayed. Praise God!

I am sure it was shared humbly. I am certain Mordecai shared their plan with shaking and trembling. I am sure he understood how crazy it sounded and how foolish they would look. Yet they fasted anyway. They set themselves to fast and pray and believed for God to move. They postured their lives in fasting and prayer with a confidence that God would make a way.

You have to remember this—you always look and sound crazy until God comes through!

You have to remember this—you always look and sound crazy until God comes through! You will always be counted as crazy until He provides. You will always be considered foolish until God really moves. You will always be criticized as fanatical until God makes a way. You will most times be counted out and looked upon as ridiculous until God does what He said He was going to do! So, here in the hostility and uncertainty of their situation and surroundings, they set themselves to fast and pray.

They fasted and they prayed, and God delivered a nation. They fasted and they prayed, and God granted them favor with the king. They fasted and they prayed, and God routed all of their enemies and adversaries in the land. They fasted and they prayed, and what the enemy intended to construct and use toward their demise was the very thing that came crashing down on all of his desires. This is the power of our God. This is the beauty of His ways.

Have you considered that everything about your life could be the canvas upon which God has been painting and preparing you to fulfill His purposes?

All of this sounds wonderful when considered in the context of Esther's life, but what about yours? Have you considered that everything about your life could be the canvas upon which God has been painting and preparing you to fulfill His purposes? Your beginnings could be a divine setup for God's glorious ending and outcomes in your life that will affect many others, and potentially nations.

All of what you have been through could be the exact funnel God has been sifting you through to move you into certain positions and places so He can use you in a mighty way. Your life, like Esther's, could be the answer for the generation that you are a part of. Your life, like Esther's, could be what God has been forming to see deliverance come to a nation, to a region, to a city, to a school campus, to a household!

In the time that divine wisdom was needed to know how to navigate the uncertainties they were facing, they fasted. Have you considered that it may be through your next fast that God may release divine wisdom on how to navigate situations that are before you to bring breakthrough and deliverance? Have you thought about the fact that you may be a fast away from receiving the necessary favor with certain people in authority and powerful positions to see certain desires that are in God's heart fulfilled?

May you be one that seizes the moment in your day and postures your life before God in fasting to see His desires fulfilled.

You could be so close to receiving the necessary blueprint and navigation instructions on how to make your way through the complexity of certain seasons of attack and a heightened sense of the enemy's desires against your own life, a people group, a nation. This is all possible, and it is all possible for you.

May we not cast off the foolishness of fasting because of the lack of appeal culturally or militarily. May you be one that seizes the moment in your day and postures your life before God in fasting to see His desires fulfilled.

It is important to see that Esther's resolve for them to all posture themselves in fasting over those three days brought a much-needed change to a governmental order that had been issued. A nation saw the decree of a king get overturned through their efforts in fasting and prayer.

We can see the tide turn in favor of what is on God's heart when God's people humble themselves to fast and pray.

What devastating decree has been issued nationally that you believe God can overturn? What governmental policy has been undertaken that you know is not in alignment with God's heart? If Esther's situation does anything, it should provoke us to believe that we can posture our lives in similar fashion today to fast and pray and see God come crashing into the governmental structures and systems of our day.

We can experience the overturning of demonic influence. We can see the tide turn in favor of what is on God's heart when God's people humble themselves to fast and pray. All things are possible to those who believe!

Esther's life is a great example of how God works through our yes in the place of fasting. Because Esther postured her life in fasting and prayer, it became a weapon in the hand of God. God used Esther's yes to fast and pray as a way to defeat the desires of the enemy and deliver an entire nation of people. However, there is another incredible part of Esther's story that we will save for a later chapter, "Intervention and Activation," in which we discuss the power of her declaration, "If I perish, I perish." For now, though, let us move on to another great example of a weapon in the hand of God.

CHAPTER 5

REFORMERS, REVOLUTIONARIES, AND REVIVALISTS

Daniel

Our introduction into Daniel's life is a little extreme, at least when compared to the luxuries and freedoms that we enjoy in the Western world. Daniel's life was chosen for a very dark moment. God planted Daniel right in the middle of turmoil and hostility.

It is important to realize that you have been strategically selected by God for the moment you are living in. Your generation is not an accident; it is not coincidental by any means. God was very deliberate in planting your life into the time that you are alive. You have to look around at all of the complexity and the potential challenges and think to yourself, "God, you chose me for right here, right now."

When God considered all of what would be happening in the world during the time that you are alive, He thought of you as a solution. When He thought of answers, He thought of you. When He thought about break-through, He thought about you. When He thought about making a way for the Gospel to be advanced and His power to be demonstrated, He thought about you. You are not accidentally placed; you are strategically assigned!

You have been strategically selected by God for the moment you are living in.

In the opening of Daniel chapter 1 we find that God's chosen people have been overtaken. The Lord has handed over the people of Israel into captivity under the wicked King Nebuchadnezzar and allowed them to experience exile into Babylon. Daniel is a younger man that is a part of this tragedy, amongst many others. These are the details that we are given at the very beginning of what is Daniel's introduction.

Nebuchadnezzar searches throughout the exiles for younger men that he can train to serve in his kingdom.

Daniel and some of his friends are selected through this process and immediately brought in to learn and train in the literature and language of the Chaldeans. Their names are changed to reflect the culture and people that they have been overtaken by.

You are not accidentally placed; you are strategically assigned!

They are assigned a daily rationing and portions of food from the king's table.[47] This was to be a three-year training, in hopes that they would see it through to completion and then be selected to serve in the king's personal service.

It is after this brief introduction into what life looks like for Daniel, and many others, that we learn about a peculiar request that Daniel made. Daniel made up his mind that he didn't want to defile himself with the delicacies that were provided for him by way of the king's table, or the wine that he drank. Daniel requests to be exempted from the dietary provisions so that he will not have to defile himself.

Daniel speaks to the man who is in charge of them while they are in training and requests for nothing except vegetables to eat and water to drink. After a bit of hesitation and resistance from the overseer, the Lord

---

[47] Dan 1:3-7, NASB

granted Daniel extraordinary favor and he permitted it. It began with ten days. After an examination following the ten-day period, the Bible suggests that they continued on this way for the remaining three years of training before entering into the king's personal service.

Sometimes what we need most is a new perspective to see God's purposes for where He has us.

We know that God granted to Daniel and his friends incredible abilities through spiritual imparta-tion while on their fast—knowledge and intelligence in every branch of literature and wisdom—and Daniel even understood dreams and visions of all kinds.[48] This is the beginning of a powerful story of revelatory encounter, insight and understanding, and protection for Daniel.

Daniel was set up to succeed in what could have been perceived as a losing situation. Sometimes what we need most is not a way out of where we are, but rather a new perspective to see where we are, so that we can lock into God's purposes for where He has us.

As for every matter pertaining to wisdom and understanding that the king examined them in, Daniel is known as one that has abilities that are ten

---

[48] Dan 1:17, NASB

times superior to the rest of the magicians and conjurers.[49] Daniel is head and shoulders above those that are serving alongside of him. Daniel has been elevated and highlighted by God to fulfill specific purposes in the nation that he has been brought into.

The book of Daniel gives us information about his life and how he serves during the lifetime of four different kings: Nebuchadnezzar, Belshazzar, Darius, and Cyrus. In each of these seasons of Daniel's life we find God distinguishing him from among all of his peers and contemporaries, elevating him to places and positions with great influence, and helping him to navigate through the complexities that are befalling his own life and those surrounding him through revelatory encounters and insights.

As we continue to journey through Daniel's life, we find that there are specific things about Daniel that mark him. He has dreams and night visions. He is filled with wisdom and understanding. He is able to understand and interpret dreams and visions of all kinds. There are angelic messengers sent to provide counsel for him. Daniel is living a life that is full of experience in and with God, and it is greatly needed. It is not a luxury, it is a necessity for how God will use him.

---

[49] Dan 1:20, NASB

By Nebuchadnezzar Daniel is promoted to be ruler over the whole province of Babylon and chief prefect over all the wise men of Babylon.[50] During the reign of Belshazzar he is noted to carry illumination, insight, and wisdom like the wisdom of the gods. An excellent spirit, knowledge and insight, interpretation of dreams, explanation of enigmas, and solving of difficult problems were all found in Daniel.[51]

During the days and reign of Darius, Daniel distinguished himself among the commissioners and satraps because he possessed an extraordinary spirit, and the king planned to appoint him over the entire kingdom. The commissioners and satraps tried to find a way to bring accusation against Daniel in regard to governmental affairs. But they could find no ground of accusation or evidence of corruption, inasmuch as he was faithful, and no negligence or corruption was to be found in him. It was then decided that the only way to trap Daniel would be if it were connected to his commitment and faithfulness to his god.[52]

Let's pause for a moment and consider the way that Daniel lives. The only thing that you can possibly find to be wrong with someone has to be fabricated by making the way that they walk in faithful devotion

---

[50] Dan 2:48, NASB
[51] Dan 5:11-12, NASB
[52] Dan 6:2-5, NASB

to their God a crime. Wow, it is amazing to consider what God is doing in Daniel's life. Daniel is placed in the lion's den after they create a crime out of his faithful devotion to his God and his unwillingness to compromise in the face of penalty.

Once they realize that Daniel is alive in the lion's den, Darius decrees that in all the dominion of his kingdom men are to fear and tremble before the God of Daniel. Daniel's commitment to posture himself before the Lord and live in faithful accountability to God created the way for God to break in and exalt His name in a nation.

The book of Daniel is broken up into parts. The first couple chapters give us a progressive narrative of Daniel's life. This is the first six chapters, from King Nebuchadnezzar to King Cyrus. Then in chapter 7 we receive a shift in what is being communicated.

Beginning with chapter 7 through the close of the book with chapter 12 we receive insight into encounters and visitations that Daniel was having throughout his life, during the period that is specified in the first couple of chapters. This is important to understand. Over the course of Daniel's life, we have the privilege to perceive that fasting played an integral role.

In chapter 1, during the reign of Nebuchadnezzar, Daniel makes the decision to not defile himself, which looked like a self-initiated dietary modification. It is a fast—of only vegetables to eat and water to drink. Initially ten days before observation, and then implied a continuation for a total of three years.

Then in chapter 9, during the first-year reign of Darius, after reading the word of the Lord prophesied by the prophet Jeremiah, we find Daniel fasting again.

Every season, regardless of situation, Daniel was found fasting and praying. Only this time it doesn't provide us with any insight whatsoever into what kind of fasting he was actually doing. Verse 3 says, "So I gave my attention to the Lord God to seek Him by prayer and supplications, with fasting, sackcloth and ashes."[53]

And finally, in chapter 10, during the third year of King Cyrus, Daniel is fasting again. This time Daniel says, "In those days, I, Daniel, had been mourning for three entire weeks. I did not eat any tasty food, nor did meat or wine enter my mouth, nor did I use any ointment at all until the entire three weeks were completed."[54]

Daniel lived a fasted life. All of what we are able to glean from in a public sense from chapters 1 to 6 in his life was backed by a powerful life of consecration. Daniel hid himself in God with prayer and fasting.

---

[53] Dan 9:3, NASB
[54] Dan 10:2-3, NASB

This cannot be overlooked when considering the magnitude of Daniel's life and his testimony. Daniel's public navigation was infused by personal revelation through a fasted life. Every season, regardless of situation, Daniel was found fasting and praying.

One of the great facts of the story of Daniel's life is this—God planted a man as an immigrant in a pagan empire and caused him to thrive on a political platform. From the onset of Daniel's introduction, it may seem, according to the details that introduce him, that his life is being set up for extreme trial.

Daniel should've been one that just hoped to barely survive under the hostile circumstances of captivity. Yet, in the midst of a terrible situation God had a consecrated man that He could trust and lead. Daniel's setting didn't determine his devotion. God elevated Daniel under the reign of wicked kings that didn't serve his God. God gave Daniel wisdom to carry himself in powerful and influential places.

Daniel's setting didn't determine his devotion.

I believe that Daniel's life is an invitation. Of the many things that it is, it is an invitation for those of you who may feel the tug upon your heart into a political sphere. I understand that there have been many excuses throughout as to why it would be impossible to handle yourself in a political sphere of influence in a way that would honor God and bring Him glory, but Daniel obviously didn't buy into those same skeptics and critics.

It is an invitation to those of you who may feel as if the Lord is leading you abroad, into another country and culture. Daniel was essentially a missionary, not by his own choosing to get up and go, but by God's design to plant him in the empire of a nation of people that needed to be reached through the experience of exile. Daniel allowed the Lord to lead him and raise him up in a cultural situation that wasn't his own.

Daniel's life invites us into a beautiful place of consecration to God through fasting and praying.

It is an invitation for those of you who may have thought that circumstantially you might not have been dealt the best hand to set yourself up to succeed where you are, or where God is leading you. Daniel shows us that what matters most is not complaining about the hand that you were dealt, but rather identifying God's purpose in the midst of it and how He will lead you to play those cards. Daniel could have very easily embraced the voice of reason that would've told him that because of his tragedy God would no longer be able to use him in a great way.

Daniel's life invites us into a beautiful place of consecration to God through fasting and praying. Daniel is giving counsel to kings. Daniel is leading the wise men of a nation. Daniel is opening doors to promotion for other men of God in his life.

Daniel's story wasn't going to be one of him buckling under the pressure and the seemingly impossible narrative that he had been brought into. Through Daniel's life, God was able to shake a kingdom, influence kings, and shape history. Daniel's life is a great reminder that if we will choose to not make excuses for what we are facing that God has the potential to be glorified in a great way.

And Others

There are so many incredible examples throughout the history of the Scriptures of men and women that have given themselves over to God in the place of fasting and prayer and have seen God do incredible things. The goal is not to create some fanfare rockstar complex for those whose lives we glean from in themselves, but to be provoked into and onto greater places of loving Jesus and giving over more of our hearts to Him through the example of what we may see and experience in their lives.

These were people that were completely normal yet gave themselves over to God in a way that seemed to be abnormal, and God used their willingness and obedience to fulfill His purposes. There are many others that we, for the sake of time, will not highlight in great depth as the others.

Ezra

We must remember Ezra, who proclaimed a fast to seek God's protection from the enemy as he and the people were set to journey from the river Ahava to Jerusalem. Ezra writes, "Then I proclaimed a fast there at the river of Ahava, that we might humble ourselves before our God to seek from Him a safe journey for us, our little ones, and all our possessions." He continues with, "So we fasted and sought our God concerning this matter, and He listened to our entreaty."[55]

God's protection came to Ezra and his group as they were traveling throughout the land. The enemies were unable to touch them as they were passing by. Ezra recounts the scenario in saying, "We set out from the Ahava River on the twelfth day of the first month to go to Jerusalem. We were strengthened by our God, and He kept us from the grasp of the enemy and from ambush along the way."[56] There is supernatural protection from enemies when we set ourselves to fast.

---

[55] Ezra 8:21, 23, NASB
[56] Ezra 8:31, CSB

Jonah

We would have to remember Jonah. Jonah finally heads into the wicked city of Nineveh, in obedience to God, to preach to them. Jonah cries out in their streets and preaches that in forty days their great city will be overthrown. The Bible says that at hearing the words of Jonah, "Then the people believed in God; and they called a fast and put on sackcloth from the greatest to the least of them. When the word reached the king of Nineveh, he arose from his throne, laid aside his robe from him, covered himself with sackcloth and sat on the ashes. He issued a proclamation and decreed that no man, beast, herd, or flock were to taste a thing. Do not let them eat or drink water. But both man and beast must be covered with sackcloth; and let men call on God earnestly that each may turn from his wicked way and from the violence which is in his hands."[57]

The Bible tells us that when God saw their deeds, He relented from the calamity that He declared He would bring upon them. Our point here in remembering Jonah is not because he himself was found fasting, but that God used him to bring the word of the Lord that pierced the hearts of an entire city and they entered into a fast.

---

[57] Jonah 3:4-8, NASB

The preaching of Jonah is what was used as the catalyst for an entire city to turn to God in fasting, prayer, and repentance—a whole city! May God do it again in our day; raise up men and women who carry the word of the Lord to penetrate the hearts of cities and regions to see repentance and revival.

Joel

We mustn't forget the prophet Joel, whose heart burned after he received the word of the Lord. Joel surveyed the land in his day and determined that in the face of darkness and compromise there was one solution—it was time to sound the trumpet and declare a fast![58] Joel called for a holy assembly, a gathering of the elders and all the inhabitants of the land to the house of the Lord to cry out on behalf of the land.

Joel declared God's heart to the people that it was time to return to the Lord with all of their hearts, with fasting, weeping, and mourning. Joel issued a clarion for people to rend their hearts and not just their garments.[59] It is with Joel that our hearts are seized with his profound prophetic utterances that, "In the last days I will pour out my Spirit upon all flesh; And your sons and daughters will prophesy,

---

[58] Joel 2:15, NASB
[59] Joel 2:12-13, NASB

your old men will dream dreams, your young men will see visions."[60]

Let us not consider the way that God will grip the heart of a man to initiate a corporate fast to be insignificant. Joel is easily seen as a burning torch, blazing the prophetic trail for the real need of the hour: brokenness, fasting, repentance, and restoration. Do not undermine the desires that God may place in your heart to hold holy assemblies on behalf of the land. Do not turn away from the nudging of your heart to sound the trumpet and declare a fast in the midst of the congregation. May God raise up men and women in our day who would prophetically lead people to rend their hearts and not just their garments!

May God raise up men and women in our day who would prophetically lead people to rend their hearts and not just their garments!

John the Baptist

There would be no way to forget John the Baptist. John's life was completely given over to God in the wilderness from an early age until his time of appearing.[61] The Lord strategically pulled John's life from all

---

[60] Joel 2:28, NASB
[61] Mark 1:4, NASB

of the religious systems and privileges of his day as he followed Him in obedience into hiddenness and obscurity. John was a man of fasting and prayer.[62] John's life of brokenness and dependency made him a doorway for God's freedom and deliverance to come to a nation.

John arose out of the wilderness with a fiery message of repentance, especially to the religious and the Pharisees. John sparked a wilderness revival with a fresh revelation of Jesus as the Bridegroom. John's life was set upon preparing a way for the coming of the Lord! But John's life had been prepared in the place of fasting.

John gave his life to God in brokenness and fasting.

John's life, formed by fasting, gave way to the revealing of Jesus in his generation. John gave his life to God in brokenness and fasting and a generation had the privilege to feast upon the revealing of Jesus through his life. It is John that declares, "He must increase, and I must decrease."[63]

May it be again in our day, Lord, that a people would completely give themselves over to You in brokenness and dependency, and that You would bring a clear and powerful revelation of Jesus into the

---

[62] Matt 11:18, NASB
[63] John 3:30, CSB

earth in this generation. May You raise up a people who would prepare the way for the Lord with their hearts turned to You in surrender. Put holy fire on a generation of forerunners whose anthem would be, "Behold, the Lamb of God!"[64]

Oh, that we would hear all of this with fresh ears and that the Holy Spirit would give us soft hearts to receive God's desires. We too can have our hearts burn in surrender to God in fasting and prayer, hiddenness and obscurity, with a Spirit-birthed jealousy for a great revealing of Jesus in our generation! May God answer again and bring about on the earth an unleashing of those whose lives have been completely swallowed up in His heart and His purposes to declare, "Behold the Lamb!"

I hope it becomes clear through these examples of people that God used in powerful ways to shake their generation, that they were not giving themselves to God so they could become great; they were giving themselves to God so that His great name could be made known.

Shaking your generation and shaping history is not about you; it's all about Jesus. It's not about you becoming famous, or more popular than you are right now. It has absolutely nothing to do with the relational

---

[64] John 1:29, NASB

circle that you may have always desired to be a part of. It's not about you gaining great wealth just for the sake of becoming rich and creating a life of comfort. It's not for you to become the most well-known and recognized pastor or platform minister. Even if any of these things happen along the way, they are never to be considered as our primary motivations.

We must allow the Holy Spirit to intensely deal with our hearts and make us content with loving Jesus, and then from being wholly satisfied there, giving Him a place to do whatever it is that He wants to do. He is enough. Loving Him is the reward.

We must allow the Holy Spirit to intensely deal with our hearts and make us content with loving Jesus.

If any of those other things ever become a part of the equation as something that is in God's heart or plan for us, then may we steward all of it well, with innocence and excellence.

Seeing God use our lives to shake everything around us is great. However, there must also be a cry within us that desires to see God shake everything within us. I want to shake cities and see nations changed, but I also want to see God shake my heart and have my own life changed. Just because the first is happening doesn't always mean the latter is happening. That is one of the reasons that a fasted life is so necessary. It is continually working on us and empowering us to bring our lives subject to the loving rule of Jesus. We will continue this in the next chapter.

CHAPTER 6

AVOIDANCE AND MASTERY

"I have been crucified with Christ; and it is no longer I who live, but Christ lives in me; and the life which I now live in the flesh I live by faith in the Son of God, who loved me and gave Himself up for me."[65]

As believers in Jesus, we must give fasting its proper placement and function in our lives. Fasting is a part of our discipleship as followers of Christ. Fasting, as a devotional expression of a life lived in hunger for Jesus, knowing Jesus, and being conformed to the

---

image of Jesus, must be seen correctly through the lens of Jesus' desire. It is Jesus' desire that we fast. Period. There is no avoidance to that statement for the lover of Jesus, or more importantly, the beloved of Jesus. His immense love for us calls our lives into loving surrender in the place of fasting.

The offering up of our appetite to Jesus is a violent act of war to the natural man and all of his desires.

In fasting we find the offering up of our natural appetites to Jesus. This is incredibly simple and practical, yet powerful in its implications. The offering up of our appetite to Jesus is a violent act of war to the natural man and all of his desires. Whether you are aware of it at this point or not, there is a war being waged on behalf of your surrender. The war is between the Spirit and the flesh.

Your flesh was accustomed to having its way up until the point of your salvation and the deposit of the Holy Spirit into your life. There was no real conflict. The war had not yet been waged upon its governance. However, in light of your coming into a bright and beautiful revelation of Jesus as the Son of God and the reality of the glorious outpouring of the Holy Spirit, things are different now. Now there is a fight. Now there is a war.

One of the supreme goals of the working of the Holy Spirit in you is to lead you into greater places of submission to Jesus. Your surrender to Jesus, and greater depths of that surrender, is being jealously sought after by the working of the Spirit in your heart and life right now. This is important to understand. This beautiful truth will help to frame in much of what you go through. The Holy Spirit is doing many things in your heart as we speak, but I promise you, one of those things is this— working to bring you into greater surrender to Jesus.

One of the supreme goals of the working of the Holy Spirit in you is to lead you into greater places of submission to Jesus.

You may have surrendered all things to Jesus at the point of your salvation, your conversion experience, but now the Holy Spirit is taking what was confessed on that day and making it real in a day-to-day way in your heart and life. The Holy Spirit is bringing you into the surrender that you declared on the day when you asked Jesus to become the savior of your life.

Regardless of whether or not you felt that moment to be incredibly supernatural in feeling, there are great implications to our allegiance being pledged to Jesus and the effects of that pledge now upon our own desires and the war of our flesh to be the controlling or dominant influence in our life.

In speaking about the source of this conflict, Paul wrote it this way to the believers in Ephesus, "And you were dead in your trespasses and sins, in which you formerly walked according to the course of this world, according to the prince of the power of the air, of the spirit that is now working in the sons of disobedience. Among them we too all formerly lived in the lusts of our flesh, indulging the desires of the flesh and of the mind, and were by nature children of wrath, even as the rest. But God, being rich in mercy, because of His great love with which He loved us, even when we were dead in our transgressions, made us alive together with Christ (by grace you have been saved), and raised us up with Him, and seated us in heavenly places in Christ Jesus."[66]

Of all of the wonderful things that Paul reveals and communicates throughout the book of Ephesians, this section in chapter 2 is of great importance and creates the context to the point that we are making here. Paul states that at one point in their life they were just like everyone else, subjected to the prince of the power of the air. At one point in their life there was an influence that was seeking to govern their existence, and it was

---

[66] Eph 2:1-6, NASB

leading them in very specific ways—the indulgence of the desires of their flesh and mind. The indulgence of their flesh and mind is what was being used as fuel to motivate their disobedience.

This spirit working in the sons of disobedience is the influence of the powers of the air—we will talk more about the influence of the powers of the air in the next chapter—but for now, suffice it to say that disobedience can be understood, according to the revelation which Paul is communicating, as the yielding to the influence from the powers of the air in satisfying our lives through fleshly desires, both mind and flesh.

Paul doesn't offer a middle ground here. There isn't a safe place to hide for those who don't like what considering the implications of Paul's communication offers. Either you are a part of the crowd that is being influenced through the powers of the air, being held hostage as a captive to your own fleshly satisfaction; or by God's great love for you, you have come alive to Christ, thus now surrendering all of your life to Him and being jealously brought under His leadership through the influence of His Spirit which is currently at work in you.

Do you see the beautiful contrast being made here? Can you begin to peel back the layers and understand the war that is being waged for who and what will have the dominant place of influence in your heart and life?

What amazing love that has freed us from the bondage of being a prisoner to self-satisfaction. What a great redeeming love that has transferred us out of the darkness and bondage of only having us and what we want to think about and has now translated us into the light. Now we can clearly see the bright-burning radiant face of the lover of our souls, Jesus the Son. Now we can offer our lives in loving devotion to Him who has captured our allegiance by His own blood.

The Holy Spirit in us fuels our surrender to Jesus.

Jesus has made a way for our lives to be free from the influence of the powers of the air. God has made us alive in Christ and seated us in heavenly places in Him. We can, and are, to now live by and through the influence of Jesus' Spirit living in us. The Holy Spirit in us fuels our surrender to Jesus.

It is important that we frame things in correctly so that other truths can have their proper placement and function. In the book of Romans, Paul references this war being waged within and the conflict that is present on the inside due to the reality of two natures, which both carry influence. There is a nature that is sinful, born of the flesh; and there is a new nature, that of the Spirit, made real in us through our yielding to God and coming alive to Christ.

There is a battle happening. Paul writes in Romans chapter 7, "I have discovered this principle of life—that when I want to do what is right, I inevitably do what is wrong. I love God's law with all of my heart. But there is another power at work within me that is at war with my mind. This power makes me a slave to the sin that is still within me. Oh, what a miserable person that I am! Who will free me from this life that is dominated by sin and death? Thank God! The answer is in Jesus Christ our Lord."[67]

The Holy Spirit helps us to conquer desires within us that are opposed to the leadership of Jesus.

God in His great love for us has freed us from the captivity to sin. We are no longer sons of disobedience. We are no longer rebels. Our fight is no longer to establish our own way, our own cause, the satisfaction of ourselves through the desires of our flesh and mind—we have been set free! Now the Holy Spirit working within us is helping to bring our lives subject to the loving rule of Jesus and His desires for us.

The Holy Spirit helps us to conquer desires within us that are opposed to the leadership of Jesus. The Holy Spirit is working in us in a powerful way to help us conquer and master our desires, to where we are

---

[67] Rom 7:21-25, NLT

actually transformed and made to be something new, and not just suppressing them altogether and pretending that we have changed. The Holy Spirit is helping you to master the desires of your flesh and make them subject to Jesus. The goal here is mastery and not just avoidance, for becoming a master of avoidance is not the same as mastering your desires and being transformed.

Becoming a master of avoidance is not the same as mastering your desires and being transformed.

Suppression is not real freedom. The act of suppressing things that are still very alive and active within us, and then pretending that they don't exist, or worse, just becoming a great cover-up artist, is not real freedom at all—it is greater bondage. Denying what you honestly recognize is still alive is not freedom. Suppression is not freedom; transformation is freedom.

The total displacement of certain desires through the transformative power of the Holy Spirit's work within us is the hope that we have in becoming changed and being free. We are not to suppress who we once were and call that freedom. We are being changed. We are being transformed. We are becoming more like Christ. Herein lies our real hope. Herein is the real glory of the work of the Holy Spirit within you.

The Holy Spirit is not empowering suppression, but transformation! Hear me, the Holy Spirit is not helping you in the pursuit of suppressing desires attached to your old nature. The Spirit is seeking to expose them and transform them, thus making you something new and no longer enabling the old to live—it must die, and the Spirit provides the death certificate.

The Holy Spirit is helping you to master your flesh. Please do not read this and let it sound odd to you. By bringing your life subject to the desires of Jesus and His loving rule, the intention here is one of mastery and not just avoidance. This means that Jesus' desires rule your life. This means that you are no longer a captive to what your flesh and your mind think is most satisfying; the will of Jesus and His desires for you is what now govern your satisfactions. This is vitally important and can beautifully be seen in the place and practice of fasting.

You can succeed in avoiding food for an entire fast and still not succeed in God's desired goals in fasting.

The goal of fasting is not simply to avoid food for short or prolonged periods of time. Fasting is defined as abstaining from food or particular foods. Yes, I understand that. But there is a goal in fasting that digs much deeper into the heart and life than the simple avoidance of food. You can succeed in avoiding food for an entire fast and still not succeed in God's desired goals in fasting.

Fasting is a multifaceted devotional expression that God uses as a tool to carve out His work and desires in your life. One of the desires that God has for you is mastery. It would be very easy during fasting to just simply avoid food the entire time and then create a checkmark on your list of devotional objectives and chalk it up as a success. However, when peeling back some of the layers of what is actually happening during times of fasting, it requires a little bit more investigation.

The avoidance of desires is very different than the mastery of desires.

Staying away from food is not the only goal. Suppressing your cravings for a specific time period is not what the definition of success should be. We are bringing our lives subject to Jesus and seeking His rule in our hearts. We are contending by the Spirit for mastery and not just avoidance.

You can avoid desires. You can set them aside and then do a great job at pretending that they no longer exist. However, the avoidance of desires is very different than the mastery of desires. The point here is not to hide from food for the fear of caving under the pressure of cravings that you don't believe you have the power to deal with. But this is how most spend their time in fasting.

Can't answer phone calls for lunch appointments. Have to keep away from cooking meals for my children while on this fast. Don't dare invite people over for meals. I know this may produce a smile or warrant a laugh, but the point is clear. During times of fasting we can easily dodge the very issue that God longs to confront.

God wants to expose our lack of real power when under pressure through various temptations due to a lack of real transformation in specific areas of our heart and life. Not just for the sake of exposure, but also for us to recognize our desperate need to fall into His loving arms to receive His transformation. His love changes us, but we have to allow Him in to love us, satisfy us, and ultimately free us!

During times of fasting we can easily dodge the very issue that God longs to confront.

Avoidance doesn't seem like real hope to me. The goal is, by the Spirit, to allow the vicious confrontation to happen that is necessary to reveal the areas of our hearts where we claim Jesus' rule yet live by our own fleshly power and governance.

We have to stop embracing excuses. I fully understand that the flesh is weak. I think we would all agree to that point without hesitation. Even the most disciplined and determined among us are still weak in comparison to the powerful operation of the Holy Spirit. Our fleshly resolve is no match for the Spirit's transformative work in our lives. For in our weakness His strength is made perfect.[68]

Has the work of the Spirit in your heart and life brought you into a powerful place of transformation where you are something different?

We must realize the goal of the work that is happening in us. Through the Holy Spirit living in you, you can master your desires and not just continue to avoid them. You can actually be free and not just pretend like you are. You can sing it. You can converse about it over your favorite latte. But are you living the reality of it?

Has the work of the Spirit in your heart and life brought you into a powerful place of transformation where you are something different? Please don't just quickly pass over what is being asked here without allowing the Holy Spirit a place to perform a thorough examination.

It is of great necessity for the lover of Jesus to live in powerful reality and not just the life of decorating an

---

[68] 2 Cor 12:9, ESV

exterior that is still suffering on the interior. Too many have been so broken for so long and not yet experienced the beauty and reality of what we are discussing here and have therefore just chosen to forego it altogether and attempt to adapt to life with the issues.

Adaption is not the same as transformation. You shouldn't be put in a position where you memorize songs about freedom that you don't get to taste for yourself. But this is the whole point. God is not holding out on you; He is longing to change you.

The goal is for Jesus' influence to be the dominant influence in your life, meaning you have become free from all of the other cravings of the flesh and mind that once held you captive. Not to say that they won't come knocking again or attempt to lure you back into and under their influence. But that you have become something new and recognize you no longer have to respond to what once controlled you in your life.

You can't live in both places at the same time. This is what I mean when I say it's time to stop it with the excuses. If we are to continue the conversation of fasting and prayer, we can't avoid this talk. The most basic offering of our natural appetite is challenging the fundamental place of leadership that our flesh has occupied. Being free unto Jesus is being free from ourselves and the influence of the powers of the air. This is what the Spirit longs to form within us.

Fasting provides the necessary crucible to expose and examine the allegiances of our hearts. Fasting peels back the covers of our confessions and highlights what is reality. Fasting reveals the ultimate authority that we have subjected our lives to. Do I really think that all of this is possible or happening during times of simply modifying our diet day to day or abstaining from food altogether? I absolutely do. And I pray that God would give grace for the eyes of your understanding to be opened. This is no small matter.

Fasting provides the necessary crucible to expose and examine the allegiances of our hearts.

We are having this conversation in the context of fasting and food, yet it is applicable to all of life. Fasting will directly challenge your fleshly influence through the offering up of your natural appetite to the Lord, yes. But it will also challenge all of the other influences that have formed in your heart through your mind and flesh that are not fully subjected to Christ. All of what needs to be challenged and transformed gets revealed during times of fasting. We must be discerning, as the processing of our hearts and lives happens during times of fasting.

Our real transformation depends on our yielding to the work of the Spirit within us. It is necessary for us to experience God's transformation in our lives so we can become brokers of it in the earth unto the lives of others. Our freedom from the influence and hostility of the powers of the air is no small thing; it is a Kingdom work in our lives. We are ambassadors of another kingdom. We are representatives of a great King!

As we close this chapter we will look to the words of Paul to the Galatians, "I have been crucified with Christ; and it is no longer I who live, but Christ lives in me; and the life which I now live in the flesh I live by faith in the Son of God, who loved me and gave Himself up for me."[69]

All of what needs to be challenged and transformed gets revealed during times of fasting.

Our life is no longer being lived solely unto the satisfaction of our own desires, but rather because of our surrender to Jesus, we are being made into something brand new, a new creation, bound to Him rather than bound to ourselves. There is great jealously on the part of the Spirit within us to make us more like Jesus, but yet even this statement has serious and very real implications to it as well, much of what we will discuss in our next chapter.

---

[69] Gal 2:20, NASB

CHAPTER 7

TRANSFORMATION AND CONFRONTATION

"I will no longer talk much with you, for the ruler of this world is coming, and he has nothing in Me."[70]

I n the previous chapter we set in motion the thought that fasting is not just simply about the avoidance of food and the suppression of our natural desires. Rather, God, by His Spirit, is working in us, not to empower the suppression of who we are, but unto the powerful transformation of who we are.

---

[70] John 14:30, NKJV

Fasting is about transformation and not just suppression. You can hide who you are without changing who you are. We can learn little behavioral techniques that provide us the ability to not have the hard confrontation with things that need to be changed and just learn to cover them up with different techniques, images, gimmicks and façades. But this is the whole point.

Your life becomes a weapon of confrontation when you yield in the place of fasting and allow God to conform you to the image of Jesus.

Thank God for His amazing grace and wonderful mercy to conform our lives to the image of Jesus! We are being made more like Christ, and fasting is one of the aggressive tools and accelerated ways that God the Father uses to accomplish that goal in us.

Fasting must be understood in terms of transformation. When seen this way, we can understand the powerful potential for fasting to make us like Jesus, and then allow our lives to become a powerful weapon in the hand of God. Your life becomes a weapon of confrontation when you yield in the place of fasting and allow God to conform you to the image of Jesus.

Confrontation? Yes, exactly. Being conformed to the image of Jesus is not just simply about learning to mimic certain behaviors or adopt certain language. You can do these things without actually being changed. You can do the whole external Jesus thing and never actually have a powerful change of what is on the interior. We want what is on the inside changed, and not just what is done on the outside modified. This takes time, and it takes a real work of the Holy Spirit in you.

God's desire for your life is to be conformed to the image of Jesus. Paul communicates what is in God's heart for you in the book of Romans when he writes, "For those whom He foreknew, He also predestined to become conformed to the image of His Son, so that He would be the firstborn among many brethren."[71] Being conformed to the image of Jesus must be understood correctly for the real implications of this statement to hit as hard and go as deep as is necessary.

God's desire for your life is to be conformed to the image of Jesus.

We live in a day where images have become ultimate and have taken center stage. Social media has created a world filled with images that gain our attention and consume us on a daily basis. The issue is not that we have become oversaturated with images, although there are things to work through here. But we have become

---

[71] Rom 8:29, NASB

accustomed to images that may not necessarily present what is actually real.

Photos can be modified. Images can be worked on and tweaked so a larger audience sees what I want them to see and not what is actually real. Filters can be applied. Touch-ups for things that we are not satisfied with can happen. We can adjust the image so we can post it and feel better about what we are giving the rest of the world to view.

Being conformed to the image of Jesus will cost you everything.

Well, all of this sounds great for social media, and other places where these principles apply, but this isn't how a real life in and by the Spirit works. You don't get to make the necessary modifications and apply filters to your walk with Christ. We have to deal with what needs to be changed. We have to confront the areas that need transformation and not just learn the necessary tools to fabricate the image that we want everyone to see, and potentially like, or subscribe to.

Being conformed to the image of Jesus will cost you everything. There is great work involved in penetrating down into the core of your heart and life and actually bringing powerful change to the real you. The real me? Yes, the real you. Not the you that knows how to manage the look and feel that you give to different crowds. The real me? Yes, not the you that can do well to keep your Christian life intact by your own fleshly initiative and wisdom.

There is a need to change the real you, what is actually hidden and happening beneath the surface. Beneath the surface of what you have learned to do and say over time is a you that God lovingly desires to change. And this is not to suggest that it is always a seriously negative thing. However, it doesn't have to be seriously negative to be bad and in need of real change.

The investigative processing of our hearts and lives is not up to our own estimation of what a good Christian should look like, sound like, feel like—we want to be like Jesus. We want to bear His actual nature. We want to be made into His image. You can learn how to do things

The danger of our day is that men and women can learn how to be Christian without clinging to Christ.

that Jesus did in a behavioral way without actually bearing His image. This is not the goal, and in fact, it is really dangerous.

The danger of our day is that men and women can learn how to be Christian without clinging to Christ. You can learn how to do things that are perceived to be godly without real dependency on God. This must change! May the Spirit break down all of our desire for independence and may we once again fall lovingly into the arms of Jesus. We must cling to Jesus in order to become more like Jesus.

Being made into His image is the work of the Holy Spirit in us, developing and forming within us the nature of Christ. The substance of His character being formed in you is what this is about. And this is what takes real work.

Your being conformed to the image of Jesus is what becomes a confrontation to powers and principalities.

You can't fake the character of Jesus. You don't have the ability to quickly manufacture the real substance of Jesus. This requires real change. Jesus' interest is not that you, apart from Him, try to be like Him the best that you know how. The real hope is found in that God is actually able to change us and not just provide the energy for us to sustain the cover-up attempts the rest of our life. Praise God!

It is important that we realize how desperately we need to be changed. Your being conformed to the image of Jesus is what becomes a confrontation to powers and principalities. I understand the strength of this statement, but you must see it.

The powers of the air are not worried about you memorizing songs. The powers of the air are not worried when you learn to recite Scripture verses. The powers of the air don't really get shaken when you get demonstrative in times of excitement. The powers of the air are shaken and broken by one thing—the nature of Jesus.

The nature of Jesus is the substance of who He is. It is the power source, if you will, of His life. His nature. His character. The actual substance and DNA of His makeup. It is important that we understand why this is so significant. If we don't understand this, then we will not have the proper lens to interpret what our life as a weapon is actually being formed towards.

In John chapter 14, Jesus makes a statement that reveals the heart of what we are discussing right now. He says, "I will not speak much more with you, for the ruler of the world is coming, and he has nothing in me."[72] Let's break this down into different pieces so we can bring proper analysis to what He is saying.

The powers of the air are shaken and broken by one thing—the nature of Jesus.

First, the ruler of the world. We understand that Jesus is talking about the influence the enemy currently has within the realm of the earth, his jurisdiction. The enemy has a specific place of authority in the earth, and it is referenced as the air. The ruler of world has come. The one who governs the powers of the air has come.

---

[72] John 14:30, NASB

This is the chief adversary of Jesus, radically opposed to Him, His ways, His Father, and the Holy Spirit.

Next, Jesus declares that although the ruler of the world is coming, He Himself is not afraid. There is no fear in Jesus. He is not moved by fearful consequence of what the authority of the adversary will be able to accomplish. Jesus is not swayed or persuaded to act in certain ways to appease the will of the one who is coming against Him. He is settled in the will of His Father.[73]

He understands fully that He is on a mission and fulfilling His Father's desires.[74] There is no one, including the ruler of the world and the powers of the air, that is taking His life from Him, for He is joyfully and willingly laying it down in His own power and on His own accord.[75] Jesus is free from fear because He is full of the Spirit. For God has not given us a spirit of fear, but of power, love, and a sound mind.[76]

The next statement that Jesus makes is powerful. He says, "for he has nothing in Me." When He says that he has nothing in Him, what He means is that there is nothing of the enemy's character that can be found in Him. Jesus is free from the influence of the

---

[73] Phil 2:7, NASB
[74] John 6:38, NASB
[75] John 10:18, NASB
[76] 2 Tim 1:7, NASB

powers of the air. There is nothing that the enemy can do to examine the life and character of Jesus in order to lay claim to something that is in Him that may belong to him.

The ways of the enemy have not gotten into the life of Jesus. Jesus is free from the distortion and the infection of the influence of the powers of the air. The enemy doesn't have any place when looking into the life of Jesus to say that He looks like him in any way, sounds like him in any way, or behaves like him in any way. There is nothing in Jesus or about Jesus that belongs to or has originated from the enemy's influence. Wow!

There is nothing in Jesus or about Jesus that belongs to or has originated from the enemy's influence.

It is the life of Jesus that is confrontational to the authority and influence of the powers of the air. The enemy and his divine rebels are hostile towards God and His ways. The enemy absolutely hates the way that God operates. He hates His character. He hates everything about Him. This is why Jesus is a confrontation to the powers of the air and the ruler of the world.

The life of Jesus, that meaning His very makeup and substance, has not been tainted by the ways or character of the enemy. We must remember that Paul tells us that, "He made Him who knew no sin to be sin on our behalf, so that we might become the righteousness of God in Him."[77] Jesus is the perfect representation of God; therefore, Jesus is a direct confrontation to the authority of the powers of the air.

God is using your life being conformed to the image of Jesus to challenge and confront the powers of the air. This is another reason why we must desperately seek to be changed. Your transformation is an act of spiritual warfare.

God is using your transformation as a weapon in His hand against the desires of the enemy.

God is using your transformation as a weapon in His hand against the desires of the enemy. It's why we must see and understand why it is so important that we are actually changed and not just pretend like we are. Parading around publicly like we are free when privately we are bound isn't helping anybody, including ourselves.

We must experience God's loving deliverance and transformation so that we can become agents and brokers of it in the earth to those around us. Our transformation becomes a confrontation to those around us. It becomes a confrontation because we become a picture of what's possible. The lie of impossibility no

---

[77] 2 Cor 5:21, NASB

longer has an authoritative place once God does it in you. But that's the point; God has to really do it in you.

Those things that we secretly give place to in our hearts will need to be dealt with before we can confront the influence of them over a city, region, or nation. John the Baptist provides for us a powerful picture here. John is a man that was pulled out of something. Removed from a religious system. His life was spent being fully given over to God in a wilderness place of joy-filled devotion.

There were many things that John was pulled out of. However, it was not just that John had his life pulled out of all of these things, but rather that all of the influence of these things was equally pulled out of John. John was not just a man that changed his address; what needed to be addressed in John had received the powerful work of God. It is not enough to just remove your life from certain things and then call that victory. You must also, by the Spirit, now allow the influence of such things to be pulled out of you.

You can be completely removed from something physically and yet be captive to its influence internally.

You can be completely removed from something physically and yet be captive to its influence internally. This makes all the difference when we consider our life becoming a confrontation. John's life had become a confrontation, because he had been pulled out of much, yes, but he had also had much pulled out of him. John was a man that was authorized because he was a man that had been transformed. And we know that Jesus described John's life as having come with fasting.[78] A life of consecration unto God coupled with fasting and prayer had much to do with making John the weapon that he had become.

The sons of Sceva also provide for us a great example of the opposite end of the spectrum to the point that we are discussing here. In Acts chapter 19 there is an issue with a man that is bound by demonic powers. The Scripture tells us that in an attempt to cast out the influence and power of the enemy in the life of the man, the sons of Sceva, who were itinerant Jewish exorcists, shouted out, "In the name of Jesus, whom Paul preaches." The evil spirit answered and said, "Jesus I know, and Paul I know, but who are you?"[79]

There was no recognition in an unseen realm for the sons of Sceva. There was no authorization from a heavenly place for them to be encouraged towards such confrontation. This is the issue; they simply believed that they could copy and paste what they had seen or heard Paul doing and that it would produce

---

[78] Matt 11:18, NKJV
[79] Acts 19:13-15, NASB

the same results. They were sadly mistaken. And not only could they not bring a proper eviction to the evil spirit, but they also were beaten badly, bloodied, and embarrassed.[80]

When it comes to hard confrontation with the powers of the air, there is only one thing that will do—the real forming of the image of Jesus in your life!

The issue is not how loud you can shout. The issue is not the powerful and performance-oriented prayers that you know to pray. The issue is not whom you have been watching and how well you can mimic their techniques. The issue is not even how close you may think you are to someone who actually carries real authority.

All of these things may work well in other places, but when it comes to hard confrontation with the powers of the air, there is only one thing that will do— walking intimately and deeply with the Lord and the real forming of the image of Jesus in your life! In the consideration of spiritual warfare there is no substitute for your being deeply connected to the Lord and the real work of transformation that has happened in you over time.

---

[80] Acts 19:13-16, NASB

These men in Acts could not cast the enemy's influence out of the life of the man they encountered. They found out very quickly that the enemy didn't care about the outward performance and hollow speech. The enemy occupied certain territory, that being the life of the man, and these men were not authorized to remove him. This is very heartbreaking to consider.

It will take the work of the Spirit in our hearts to bring the proper exposure to things we have embraced and entertained that belong to the enemy.

But what about for you? Have you considered yourself a broker of breakthrough for those around you? Have you thought about your own life and the way God may want to use you to cast out the enemy from people you may encounter? And then we must consider the enemy's influence, not just in people, but also over cities, regions, and nations.

If we are seeking to confront and evict the powers of the air over our city, region, and nation, it will take a mighty work of the Spirit within us. In order to provide the needed eviction to the hostility that is found in the air and the influence of the ruler of the world in an unseen realm, it will take the work of the Spirit in our hearts bringing the proper exposure to things we have embraced and entertained that belong to the enemy.

There must be a deep purging of heart, mindsets, and behavior for us to come to the same confidence that Jesus had to say, "The ruler of the world has come, but I am not afraid, because he does not have anything in me."[81]

---

[81] John 14:30, NASB

CHAPTER 8

PRINCIPALITIES AND POWERS

"For our struggle is not against flesh and blood, but against the rulers, against the powers, against the world forces of this darkness, against the spiritual forces of wickedness in the heavenly places."[82]

If you have fully given your life over to Jesus and pledged your allegiance to Him as King, the Bible deems that you are now an ambassador of another kingdom. You are a heavenly representative in the earth. God has delivered you from the domain of

---

[82] Eph 6:12, NASB

darkness and transferred you into the Kingdom of His beloved Son.[83]

Your life is not your own; you belong to Jesus. And your life now represents the beauty of Jesus through your yielding to the work of the Holy Spirit within you who is wonderfully and jealously forming you into the image of Jesus.

You are not just an arbitrary member of God's Kingdom, but you are a powerful ambassador. God has gone to great lengths to deliver you from the kingdom of darkness. His own life was laid down. His own blood was poured out. God made a way for you to be completely freed from the influence of, and powerful grip of, the kingdom of darkness.

It was God's own love and desire for you that brought Him to lay His life down for you. And now, through your belief in what God has done, you have been transferred into the Kingdom of His beloved Son. Praise be to God forever for His mighty work and amazing love!

You have been delivered from the kingdom of darkness. The kingdom of darkness is a real place. The kingdom of darkness has real influence. The kingdom of darkness is mentioned throughout the Bible in a variety of ways. One of those ways is the reference of

---

[83] Col 1:13, ESV

the powers of the air. It is important that we create a proper lens through which we view and interpret what the powers of the air actually are and how our lives are to be postured.

There are many references throughout the Scriptures that provide us with evidence of how real and active the powers of the air are. It would do us a lot of good if we were properly informed about this reality by being honest about what the Bible actually has to say about this subject. There are many that would consider this type of talk to be foolish. That's okay. We will allow the Bible to say what the Bible says and then labor by the Spirit in prayer for greater insight and understanding pertaining to these matters.

Our goal here will be to provide several places throughout the Scriptures where we can find references to what is commonly referred to as the powers of the air so we can create a basic understanding of its life and purpose. To dig much deeper into this subject I would highly recommend the book, *The Unseen Realm: Recovering the Supernatural Worldview of the Bible*, by Dr. Michael Heiser. It is a fantastic book with great biblical analysis and powerful insights.

So, where did the powers of the air come from? What are the intentions of the powers of the air? What are we supposed to do about it? Those are all great questions, and questions that we will seek to answer.

Let's say this to start—which should help to provide a proper frame in order for the following information to hang in its proper place—the powers of the air are determined to disrupt and destroy the unity that can be experienced between God and man, and man and man.

Where Did Powers Come From?

To answer the question, "Where did the powers of the air come from?" there is a peculiar verse in the book of Jude that oftentimes gets read right over and neglected. Jude is speaking about men who are ungodly and deny the Lord. He then references those that had been delivered out of the land of Egypt but were later destroyed for their lack of belief.

Right in this section of his writing he says, "And the angels who did not keep their proper domain, but left their own abode, He has reserved in everlasting chains under darkness for the judgment of the great day…"[84] What? Angels that left their proper place of dwelling, rebelling against God, and are now bound in chains in darkness, awaiting the day of judgment, seriously? Yes, seriously.

Have you ever heard a message on this verse? I don't think I have, and if so, it has been some really wild and off-the-wall stuff. However, that isn't the point. The

---

[84] Jude 1:6, NASB

point is that Jude is communicating to us that there are created divine beings, angels, who rebelled against God's desires and left their designated, or assigned, place of living. It is very necessary that we create a connection point for what Jude is communicating. That way it doesn't get wrapped up in our inability to interpret correctly.

The situation that Jude describes finds its context with the scenario that unfolds in Genesis chapter 6, where the Bible tells us, "Now it came about, when men began to multiply on the face of the land, and daughters were born to them, that the sons of God saw that the daughters of men were beautiful; and they took wives for themselves, whomever they chose."[85]

It goes on to tell us, "Then the LORD said, 'My Spirit shall not strive with man forever, because he is also flesh; nevertheless, his days shall be one hundred and twenty years.' The Nephilim were on the earth in those days, and also afterward, when the sons of God came into the daughters of men, they bore children to them. Those were the mighty men who were of old, men of renown."[86] This may seem a little confusing, but we will quickly attempt to address the points being made here in Genesis at the beginning of the sixth chapter.

---

[85] Gen 6:1-2, NASB
[86] Gen 6:3-4, NASB

First, the sons of God were upon the earth. Tying this back into what Jude is telling us about the angels that left their proper place of living, the sons of God here is a reference to those angelic beings. These are angelic beings that have rebelled against God and His loving leadership. These are angelic beings that have become rebels through the influence of the devil.

Jesus, in speaking about the devil, said, "I saw Satan fall like lightning from heaven."[87] This scene is described in the book of Revelation, "Now war arose in heaven, Michael and his angels fighting against the dragon. And the dragon and his angels fought back, but he was defeated, and there was no longer any place for them in heaven. And the great dragon was thrown down, that ancient serpent, who is called the devil and Satan, the deceiver of the whole world—he was thrown down to the earth, and his angels were thrown down with him."[88]

Second, is the reference to the Nephilim. These are the children born to the sons of God and the daughters of men. Just to be clear, this is not just implying what you may be thinking. It is directly stating it. The sons of God saw that the daughters of men were beautiful in appearance and desired them. Acting upon that desire they took wives for themselves and went

---

[87] Luke 10:18, NKJV
[88] Rev 12:7-9, ESV

into them. Having gone into them they bore children. These children are the Nephilim.

The New Living Translation writes the verse out this way, "They gave birth to children who became the heroes and famous warriors of ancient times."[89] These offspring of the sons of God and the daughters of men were also referenced as giants. This clearly becomes very important as you progress through the Old Testament narrative and encounter the problematic tribes where traces of the giants can be found—Amorites, Anakim, and the Zamaummim, just to reference a few.

Lastly, it is necessary to see what happens immediately after this. The Lord looks at what has happened and is greatly saddened. He is saddened because now every intent of the thoughts of the heart of man is wicked at all times. Wow, that is an overwhelmingly strong statement. What has happened to create such a crazy downward spiral in the heart of man?

Up until this point you see God pursuing man and lovingly coming after him. The issue in the garden, the sin of Adam and Eve, didn't even cause God to have such a strong perspective. But now, after the sons of God had children with the daughters of men, a new kind of wickedness entered into God's creation. This corruption is something that God sees fit to handle

---

[89] Gen 6:4, NLT

by wiping out all of creation with the flood that will overtake the earth.

Do you see what's happening here? This is something that is very serious. We cannot afford to simply undermine the implications of what these passages in Genesis are telling us. Divinity is mingling with humanity and it is producing a rebellion instead of reconciliation. We must see this for the counterfeit of God's design and overall attempt for disruption to God's plan that it is.

The enemy will always attempt to disfigure God's desires and derail His intentions.

It has always been God's desire to mix divinity with humanity, just not the way that the sons of God went after it. The enemy will always attempt to disfigure God's desires and derail His intentions. The language that Genesis uses is key. The sons of God "lusted" after the daughters of men. They "took" them for themselves. They "went" into them and had children. This is not God's way. Consider how radically opposite this is to the situation that we find in Luke's gospel when Gabriel comes to Mary.

Gabriel brings the announcement that Mary will carry a child for God, His Son. At the conclusion of their interaction Mary asks the all-important question,

"How can this be, since I am a virgin?"[90] The angel answered and said to her, "The Holy Spirit will come upon you, and the power of the Most High will overshadow you; and for that reason, the holy Child shall be called the Son of God."[91] Mary's response to all of this was to say, "Behold, the bondslave of the Lord; may it be done to me according to your word."[92] Mary's surrender is what created the intimate context for her to carry out God's desires.

God always designed divinity to get into humanity through loving surrender. Intimacy is only real when there is loving surrender. For as much as the Lord may desire intimacy with you, He will never simply take it from you by force. In fact, people get into big trouble and it is considered a crime when people forcefully take intimacy from others without consent. Mary consented through loving surrender to God and His plans; therefore, the Son of God would come into the earth God's way.

> As much as the Lord may desire intimacy with you, He will never simply take it from you by force.

The enemy and his forces, rebellious divine beings, were upon the earth in those days before and after the

---

[90] Luke 1:34, NASB
[91] Luke 1:35, NASB
[92] Luke 1:38, NASB

flood. Their influence, whether embodied by creation or disembodied, is a reality. The attempt to influence God's creation, sons and daughters, towards corruption and the complete casting off of God's leadership is the aim.

A total derailing of all that God desires is fueling all of the work of the rebel forces. It plays out throughout the entire biblical narrative. God has dealt with them and their efforts, and ultimately at the closing of this age, we will see and experience the fulness of how true the Bible tells us that is.

What Are the Intentions of Principalities?

Let's take a look at a specific passage found in the book of Daniel. In chapter 10 Daniel details an encounter he had. He was fasting and praying because he had a terrifying vision. God was gracious and sent an angelic messenger to him.

Daniel describes the scenario that took place out by the Tigris River. He alone is the one that is caught up in this moment of revelatory encounter. Daniel describes the man that appeared to him and gained all of his attention. The man in the vision is all-consuming—dressed in linen, waist girded with a belt of pure gold, a body like beryl, face like lightning, eyes like flaming torches, arms and feet like the gleam of polished bronze, and a voice like tumultuous waters.

He states that the other men that were with him didn't see the vision at all. Upon hearing the sound of his words Daniel fell on his face into a deep sleep.[93]

After this Daniel continues to detail out the encounter by saying, "Then behold, a hand touched me and set me trembling on my hands and knees. He said to me, 'O Daniel, man greatly loved, understand the words that I speak to you, and stand upright, for I have now been sent to you.' While he was speaking to me, I stood trembling. Then he said, 'Do not fear Daniel, for from the first day that you set your heart to understand, and to humble yourself before God, your words were heard; and I have come because of your words.' "[94]

Daniel has been going through a season where his life has been abounding with revelatory encounters. Some of which he had insight and understanding for, and others that he didn't. Because of a terrifying vision that he had he went into a time of fasting, praying, and humbling himself before God. God answered the cry of his heart and his desire for understanding and sent an angelic messenger to him.

This messenger communicates to him that he is one that is greatly loved by God, and as soon as he postured his life toward God this way, God released

---

[93] Dan 10:6-7, 9, NASB
[94] Dan 10:10-12, NKJV

him to come to Daniel in order to bring answers and insight. This is the point in the details of what Daniel provides for us where it all gets interesting and helps to fill in some of what we need to answer our questions about the intentions of the powers of the air.

Daniel continues to write about the angel's declaration to him, "But the prince of the kingdom of Persia withstood me twenty-one days; and behold, Michael, one of the chief princes, came to help me, for I had been left alone there with the kings of Persia."[95]

After a bit more interaction the angelic messenger closes by telling Daniel, "Do you know why I have come to you? And now I must return to fight with the prince of Persia; and when I have gone forth, indeed the prince of Greece will come. But I tell you what is noted in the Scripture of Truth. (No one upholds me against these, except Michael your prince.)"[96]

Daniel provides insights for us that are necessary to create a proper lens through which we can properly see and interpret the powers of the air. Daniel's angelic messenger from the Lord tells him that he was withheld in the heavens through the opposition of the prince of Persia for a period of twenty-one days. At this point, the Lord sent Michael, a chief prince in the

---

95 Dan 10:13, NKJV
96 Dan 10:20-21, NKJV

host of angelic beings, to contend with him against the resistance that was being experienced.

Daniel's messenger finally experiences the necessary release in order to come to Daniel and convey what is on God's heart for him, but then also knows that he must go back to stand against the prince of Persia and the prince of Greece, who he says is soon coming. He also reveals that there is none who stand with him in contending this way, except for Michael.

Through Daniel's description we understand that there is opposition in the heavens, or the unseen realm, attempting to resist God's plans and purposes. There is a host of resistance that is set up against God and what He is doing. These beings are very organized, intentional, and militant in their efforts.

There is opposition in the heavens, or the unseen realm, attempting to resist God's plans and purposes.

The prince of Persia and the prince of Greece help us to identify that there is regional territorial assignment and authority for the powers of the air. We can also connect what is revealed to us here with the situation that unfolds in the Gospels where Jesus confronts the man who had the legion in him that He cast out and into the swine.

I wrote about this in my book, *Fasting*, but just to continue with our point here, if you remember what the demons said to Jesus while this scenario was unfolding, they had a very specific request, "Also he begged him earnestly not to send them out of the region."[97]

Legion knew that there was an assigned place of authority or influence for him. A place that he, and potentially others, had been assigned to operate. This is the same idea as what is being communicated when we are given insights through Daniel's encounter.

In one episode, Daniel chapter 10, we see the conflict happening in the heavens. The resistance is not directly visible. The resistance that is unleashed is something taking place in a realm that is not visible; it is unseen to the natural eye. However,

God is victorious through any and every attempt to derail or disrupt His plans.

when we shift our focus from Daniel chapter 10 to Mark chapter 5, we see that the resistance has not just chosen to occupy a place in the heavens, in an unseen place, but that the resistance has actually gotten a place of embodiment inside of a person. We would consider this to be a situation of demonic possession, where a

---

[97] Mark 5:10, CSB

demonic spirit houses itself inside of a person and begins to influence them and animate them.

In either setting, it is key that God is victorious through any and every attempt to derail or disrupt His plans. If enemy forces want to produce resistance in the heavens, holding up God's messengers from bringing much-needed revelation and insight to sons and daughters on the ground, God dispatches more help. If enemy forces want to house themselves inside of men and women on the ground, God finds a man filled with the Holy Spirit and authority to give the necessary eviction notice.

Whether in the heavens, or here on the ground, God's will cannot be stopped.

Whether in the heavens, or here on the ground, God's will cannot be stopped. He is all-powerful. This is not some kind of back-and-forth boxing match between two prized fighters that are equal in strength and ability where you wonder through the whole fight who will come out on top at the end. It is not to be viewed that way at all. There is much resistance, for this is the purpose of the powers of the air—to disrupt what God is doing and influence His creation to completely reject Him and His ways.

What Do We Do About Principalities?

In order to answer the question, "What are we to do about the powers of the air?" let's begin with a reference that we find in Paul's writing to the church in Ephesus. Paul says, "For our struggle is not against flesh and blood, but against the rulers, against the powers, against the world forces of this darkness, against the spiritual forces of wickedness in the heavenly places."[98]

It is important that we understand what Paul is saying. He makes it clear that our fight is not against flesh and blood, meaning other people that surround us. Our fight is against those that occupy authority and influence in the unseen realm, and the influence that gets wielded against and into flesh and blood. It's not names and faces; it's spirits that influence and animate people to live out their desires by thinking and behaving like them through their influence. This is very important.

Paul has communicated earlier in the book of Ephesians that there was a time in life in which we were completely given over to this influence and that it had us totally bound. He says, "And you were dead in your trespasses and sins, in which you formerly walked according to the course of this world, according to the prince of the power of the air, of the spirit that is now

---

[98] Eph 6:12, NASB

working in the sons of disobedience. Among them we too all formerly lived in the lusts of our flesh, indulging the desires of the flesh and of the mind, and were by nature children of wrath, even as the rest."[99]

Take note that part of the intentions of the influence of the prince of the power of the air is to push you to engage the lustful desires of your flesh and mind. The influence of the power of the air is working against you and attempting to find a place of influence within you to draw you away from submission to God and His ways, by directly engaging whatever you think is best—the lustful desires of the flesh and mind. The intention here is to completely cast off the idea of being subject to God's desires and the loving rule of the Spirit in our lives.

When self becomes the center, that means that God is not.

The writing here from Paul is clear, but we must make it simple in order to understand the powerful dynamics that are being implied when it comes to the powers of the air. Paul states that the influence from the prince of the power of the air is intentioned towards you giving yourself to the desires of your flesh and your mind, whatever you think is right.

---

[99] Eph 2:1-3, NASB

Self-analyzing and my own interpreting are what determine my actions, or shape my behavioral patterns. Self becomes the center and the governor for my life. When self becomes the center, that means that God is not. This is the point. The powers of the air are strategic in their attempt to bring you to a place where you lose interest in God's leadership and are no longer willing to conform your life to His ways. The influence being wielded brings about a total rejection of whatever might think and behave like God.

By casting off God's leadership in your life, the powers of the air influence what governs your life. Your thought life and behaviors are what are being targeted here. Those things that your own mind has determined are right are what begin to be lived out regularly. You can hopefully see that there is a serious issue with this being the course that our lives begin to take. But that is exactly the point.

God's leadership and the things that He has determined to be good and right for us are our offense and our defense.

The powers of the air are bent on creating destruction for all of God's creation through the seduction they wield to derail God's influence that produces His ways in people. An utter casting off of God's ways removes the protection of our lives and creates a whirlwind of chaos, and a downward spiral for all of God's loving intentions.

God's leadership and the things that He has determined to be good and right for us are our offense and our defense. We must see it this way and not give in to the lie that we can interpret for ourselves what would be best for us when it comes to us.

Fasting is one of the great ways that God has given to us to continually make sure that our hearts are synchronized to His voice.

Our generation has done a great job at attempting to remove absolute truth. Everything is being reduced down to the desires of the individual and it is now all relative to how we feel or what we want. This is not the best way for us to live. In fact, this way puts us into more damaging scenarios that could all be avoided if we would simply surrender to God's loving leadership and take heed to His ways.

Fasting helps us to sift our hearts to identify the source of what is influencing us. Fasting is a beautiful tool that allows the light of God to shine brightly within our motivations in order to clean out those things that have gained traction within us that have not been planted or imparted by God and His Spirit.

Fasting is one of the great ways that God has given to us to continually make sure that our hearts are synchronized to His voice. His voice in us, leading and guiding us into thought patterns and behavioral patterns that align with His heart and His ways.

Even though we are saved by grace, that doesn't exempt us from the fight for what wants to gain influence in our hearts and minds. We must be aware and guard our hearts from the influence of the powers of the air. As believers, the only weapons of warfare formed against us that can gain access to our hearts are the ones that we willingly embrace.

The enemy needs your agreement in order to have authority in your heart.

Willingly embrace? You may be thinking to yourself, why would I intentionally embrace a weapon that I know has been formed against me? That's a great question, and I am glad that you asked. The enemy needs your agreement in order to have authority in your heart.

The weapons that are formed against us, or the influence from the powers of the air that seek to influence us, are never just full-out disclosed as to their full intentions in the way that it may initially come packaged. These weapons of influence are oftentimes wrapped in a way that feeds into something that sounds right or feels good to you in a situation that you are going through. This is how it gains your agreement.

It is very important that we pray through what we are experiencing and not just press into or decide what may feel or sound best in any given moment.

At the end of Ephesians chapter 4, Paul writes these words, "Do not grieve the Holy Spirit of God, by whom you were sealed for the day of redemption."[100] Grieving the Holy Spirit is something I definitely do not want to be a part of. However, it is amazing, because Paul isn't just using this as an exhortative statement and then leaving it up to our own interpretation about what this potentially means.

I have seen and heard this turned into a bunch of crazy stuff. I can tell you what he is not talking about; he is not using this verse as a way to preserve our desire for orderly church services—whatever orderly may mean to us. This isn't something intended to mean— hey, you were clapping when no one else was clapping, so you are quenching the Spirit. Or, you were singing off-key, and a little too loud, so you were quenching the Spirit.

Paul's words here are not left up to us in order to just flippantly determine how, where, when, why, or to whom we want to apply them. It is actually quite different. He gives us insight as he continues, "Let all bitterness and anger and clamor and slander be put

---

[100] Eph 4:30, NASB

away from you, along with all malice. Be kind to one another, tender-hearted, forgiving each other, just as God in Christ also has forgiven you."[101]

Paul is communicating that the things that potentially disrupt our unity, on a heart level, need to be considered and abandoned entirely. The weapons that are formed against us attempt to separate us, and therefore should be viewed and considered as the enemies that they really are.

Bitterness, anger, clamor, slander, and malice are all the seeds that give birth to devastation. All of these thoughts and emotions are sown into our hearts and minds, and we then act upon their influence in us, which leads to behaviors that are in opposition to what God is like. And herein is the problem.

Not everything that we may think or feel is right in a moment may be what God desires.

All of these ideas and conditions may be easily justified, yet need to be discerned to identify the origin of their influence. Not everything that we may think or feel is right in a moment may be what God desires. Even though you may be able to justify entertaining the thoughts or behaviors in the moment doesn't mean that what it is sourced by is right.

---

[101] Eph 4:31-32, NASB

We must aggressively pray through and allow our hearts to be sifted in order to come to proper conclusions as to what God's wisdom is and what best aligns with His heart and His ways. There have been many scenarios throughout history when people have not fully considered what was influencing their decisions and actions and have brought incredibly damaging effects upon their own lives and then countless others. We will consider this in greater detail in a chapter that lies ahead—"Transforming Nations."

Keeping our hearts exposed to God in fasting helps to identify the mindsets and behaviors within us and about us that need correcting. Just because you are completely set on believing that you are well and right doesn't always mean that you are. And not being open to acknowledging that can potentially be life altering, in a very negative way, and lead to deception, where we are given over to another influence.

Keeping our hearts exposed to God in fasting helps to identify the mindsets and behaviors within us and about us that need correcting.

We must be aware of what we allow to rule our hearts. For if we are not careful, what rules our hearts ends up ruling our lives, homes, cities, and nations. And the reverse is equally true. What we can rid from our hearts ends up becoming a powerful catalyst to help in getting rid of what has ruled our lives, homes, cities and nations.

CHAPTER 9

TRANSFORMING NATIONS

"There is a way that seems right to a person, but its end is the way to death."[102]

In the last chapter we set up a basic understanding of the powers of the air and their intentions and operations. This chapter we will give our focus to answering the question, "What would it look like if the powers of the air were dismantled and displaced over a nation?" This is an important question to consider.

Most times I feel we are contending for something but haven't taken the necessary time to consider what

---

[102] Prov 16:25, CSB

the fulfillment of what we are crying out for would actually look like. Or, we have considered what the outcome of our contention would look like and have chosen to satisfy our hearts with things that fall much below what God could actually do. The powers of the air, or powers and principalities, is one of those areas where I feel that this is most seen.

We pray for breakthrough in our home. We pray for breakthrough in our church. We pray for breakthrough in our city, in our regions, and in our nation. But, what would it actually look like if the powers and principalities that have been assigned to those areas and places were to have their influence completely dismantled?

What would be the effects upon your city or your nation if the powers and principalities that have had governing authority were to not only be confronted, but were to be displaced altogether? This is something that requires prayerful consideration and grace granted by the Spirit unto revelation.

Many times, we would be willing to settle for something that is far less than what God has in mind. This is true in a variety of ways and instances. When you consider breakthrough in your church, what exactly do you think about? What are you praying for? Do you believe that real breakthrough in your church would just be a greater injection of charismatic expression?

Would it mean that meetings would be extended and there would be gatherings every night? Does breakthrough in your church mean that just more people would attend and your idea of the ultimate attendance number would finally be fulfilled? Possibly a financial goal accomplished?

What about in a city context? Would it mean that gas prices would go down? Would it mean that businesses would open and that others would thrive? Would it mean that the crime rate would significantly decrease? Would it mean that the population in the jails and hospitals would be considerably lower?

These are all very lofty-sounding ideas and all of them fit a specific purpose or fill a certain need in an immediate way. However, things that are immediate don't always serve a purpose that is ultimate.

The potential problem with this line of thinking and being satisfied with these is that all of the questions that were just asked could be answered without any real displacing of the powers of the air. All of the things that were just mentioned in the previous question-and-answer lines wouldn't require any contending with powers and principalities in order to see their fulfillment.

There are natural ways to bring about those conclusions without confronting the influence from the powers of the air. I'm not trying to be difficult.

I just want you to see that there is a lower-level way to consider things and then there is a higher place of wisdom that requires having our hearts enlightened by the Holy Spirit to see what God sees. This enables us to understand His desires and how they fully flesh out in the complex dynamics of our life and our culture.

I live in the United States of America, so most of my experience and history have been shaped by what I have gone through as I have grown up and done life here. It isn't my intention to isolate any other nations throughout the world in the following examples that I provide, but to allow the examples to be a provocative element toward the prayerful consideration as to what it would look like where you live, in your nation.

What would it look like for the powers of the air to be dismantled and displaced over your nation? I may not necessarily have a clear-cut answer as to what it would look like in its fullest measure, but we can give a thorough examination to some of the key things that would have to be affected that have been demonically inspired and constructed over time.

Principalities and powers seek to infuse their influence into men and women so they will adhere to their agenda. The agenda of powers and principalities is to completely derail all of God's desires and to blot out His ways and leadership altogether. With this in mind, we must now weigh the severe consequences of Paul's words in Ephesians that deal with being completely given over to the lusts of our minds and flesh.

Whatever people think is best and whatever feels right is not what is best. God has established a certain set of parameters in order for creation to function according to His desires. The Bible tells us in Romans that right now all of creation groans and awaits the manifestation of the sons and daughters of God.[103] When we cast off God's ways, we experience the chaos that His loving rule is in place to protect us from.

When we cast off God's ways, we experience the chaos that His loving rule is in place to protect us from.

The chaos that ensues when God's ways and leadership are removed from the equation manifests itself in a variety of ways. But it is important to keep in mind that the powers of the air are after division, destruction, and death. Their influence is intended to divide in hostility and then conquer entirely.

Jesus said that the enemy would come to steal, kill, and destroy.[104] The enemy is not looking to create a little bit of confusion here and there. Powers and principalities are after the absolute destruction of people who bear God's image, which is all of creation.

---

103 Rom 8:19, NASB
104 John 10:10, NASB

Many things have happened over the timeline of our nation that have been demonically inspired by the powers of the air. What is most important to me at this point is to bring real understanding to our hearts. That way we can posture our lives in fasting and prayer to first contend with our own hearts to find the freedom that is necessary in any area where it may be needed, and then to contend to see real breakthrough over our nation.

Let's consider some examples of demonically inspired mindsets, movements, and constructs. We will go through them somewhat quickly, because the point isn't to give a full historical analysis, but to make major points to reveal how the desires of the enemy are fulfilled through the embrace of mindsets and behaviors that have led to the creation of entire systems that have been championed and celebrated, by even Christians at times.

Racism is an ugly truth in the history of America. Racism produced the days of slavery. It is an unavoidable blemish on the face of our nation that we must own. Regardless of where our opinion lies, it is a situation that we must examine.

Racism, at its core, is the belief that one race is superior to another race and has the right to rule others. Slavery was founded in the ideology that a person's value was determined by the color of their skin and not the image of God that they bore. Slavery was a wide-open mindset, practice, and system in our nation that brought intense suffering to African Americans and others for long periods of time.

Slavery created and celebrated division between people groups. It was designed to inflict suffering onto a specific race of people and to make them subservient. Slavery was, and is, demonically inspired, period.

Racism is demonically inspired because when sifted through the character of Jesus and the heart of God it is found to be of another source. It is a perspective and a mindset that completely gets obliterated when considered in light of God's love for His creation and the inherent value that we all possess because of God's image that we all bear as His sons and daughters.

Jesus is our pattern, He is our example, and He has shown us the way.

Racism cannot stand when held up against the pattern of the suffering servant that Paul describes in Philippians chapter 2. Jesus is our pattern, He is our example, and He has shown us the way. Paul describes it in this way, "Do nothing out of selfish ambition or conceit, but in humility regard one another as more important than yourselves. Do not merely look out for your own personal interests, but also to the interests of others. Have this attitude in you which was also in

Christ Jesus, who although He existed in the form of God, would not consider equality with God a thing to be grasped, but emptied Himself, taking the form of a bond-servant, and being made in the likeness of men. Being found in appearance as a man, He humbled Himself by becoming obedient to the point of death, even death on a cross."[105]

Racism and its outlet into slavery was the utter rejection of the suffering servant, Jesus, who rather than leveraging His own perceived entitlements chose to empty Himself and serve unto death. Slavery is in direct opposition to the idea of considering others more important than yourself. Slavery is the idea that one should be served and is therefore not willing to humble himself and serve.

Racism, and its expression into the practice of slavery, is demonic, not just because of the pain and the scars that it has produced throughout hundreds of years. Racism and the expression of it in slavery is demonically inspired because of the image of Jesus that it shatters. Slavery is released through demonic influence because of the ways of God that get destroyed when it is deployed into the earth.

Slavery wasn't just championed by those who were unbelievers. There were many professing Christians

---

[105] Phil 2:3-8, NASB

who were heavily involved throughout the history of slavery. There were even believers who used the Scriptures as a means to justify and strengthen their position as to why slavery was okay as a mindset and way of life. This is completely mind-boggling to me to consider in our day. However, don't think for one moment that this is something that only resided in the hearts of people in the past.

In our nation to this day we are still currently dealing with this demonic stronghold of racism. There are still people in our nation who believe in the superiority of race. There are still people in our nation today that seek to undermine the value in races and are intent on establishing policies and practices that would assist in creating separation, segregation, and suffering once again.

If we are not careful to tend to the matters that are at hand, history will repeat itself. It is one thing to consider the generations behind us and to criticize their perspectives and practices and to even consider what our contribution would have been should we have been alive in those days. But we have the ability right now to determine what our involvement looks like in days of conflict, and God wants to employ and deploy ambassadors into the secret place and into the public place in order to confront and dismantle the influence of these demonic powers and the operation of them in our nation.

Abortion is another situation that has been employed in the earth through demonic influence. At the heart of abortion is the issue of the reproduction of life. In a fundamental sense, abortion is the rejection of life that has been created. That's plain, and that's simple. However, we must understand that man is not the author of life. Man's passion is not what authors life. Man's willpower is not what creates life. God is the author of life. And because God Himself is the author of life, He alone ultimately reserves the right and the power to be the judge of life.

The Bible provides us with great insight as to God's heart when it comes to His creation and the life that He breathes into each one of His children. "I am fearfully and wonderfully made; Wonderful are your works; my soul knows it very well."[106] "I knew you before I formed you in your mother's womb. Before you were born, I set you apart and appointed you as a prophet to the nations."[107] The Bible is clear that God is that One that says yes to life and forms it Himself.

There have been tens of millions of babies aborted over the past decades. The number of little ones that didn't have an opportunity to experience life as it was

---

[106] Ps 139:14, NASB
[107] Jer 1:5, NLT

intended for them is heartbreaking and should shake our hearts to the absolute core. Abortion is an evil mindset and practice. Abortion is murder, and there is no way around that.

Abortion isn't simply the response of a person that feels their life isn't conducive to welcome a child. We must not yield our hearts to the notion that what we want or think is best is what is ultimately right.

Many times, we pick apart this discussion by providing the absolute worst of possible scenarios to justify our position. However, the worst possible scenario, as bad as it may be, doesn't justify the compromise that is participated in when engaging the practice of abortion. And, it is not the worst absolute possible scenario, statistically, that is the case the majority of the time.

We must not yield our hearts to the notion that what we want or think is best is what is ultimately right.

Abortion is evil because it is against life. God is the author of life. God is filled with life and resurrection. The enemy is bent on killing anything and everything that bears the image of God. The enemy hates reproduction because of the image bearers that it reproduces. God Himself is the one that determined that creation would bear His image. "Let us make man in Our image, according to Our likeness."[108]

God says yes to life. Those who feel they have the power to say no to the life that God has formed are in a unique position because they have ultimately determined that they are the judge of life and not God. What's interesting about this is that if the same belief they carry

The powers of the air are determined to make you feel like you are capable of being your own God.

was executed in their case, while their mother was pregnant, then they wouldn't be here in the moment to feel empowered the way that they do. This is such a terrible and sobering thought.

The definition of marriage is another issue in our day. God has defined marriage to be the union of a man and a woman. Today this is being hotly contested and distorted. The issue of love isn't one that is left up to our own interpretation. God has determined the design for love and marriage. The wants and needs felt in the moment should never be used as the proper means to redefine things that God has already established.

---

[108] Gen 1:26, NASB

What we don't understand is that by bending the rules and twisting the definitions here and there by a little bit we are actually setting the stage to cast off all restraint, open up Pandora's box, and unleash all kinds of conflict and chaos into our lives, and the earth.

The issue is not the expression of love itself and how that is interpreted. The issue that is contested is that God is the One that should get to have the final say. It is the absolute authority of God's Word that is under attack in this matter, especially when it goes against what our felt wants or desires may be in a moment. It doesn't matter if you think you should be able to do something, or even express yourself a certain way. Feelings are not to be our ultimate authority.

If the truth is offensive, it isn't the truth that needs to change—it's you.

The powers of the air are determined to make you feel like you are capable of being your own God. The powers of the air are determined to influence you and make you feel like you don't need God's definitions or boundaries because you know what is best for you and the life that you want to live. The only problem with that is that it isn't true. You don't know what's best. That's not to be insulting; it's just to speak what is right and true. If the truth is offensive, it isn't the truth that needs to change—it's you.

Same-sex marriage stops the production of life and the reproduction of image bearers. Same-sex marriage is not compatible to God's desire for our lives to be fruitful and to multiply, fill the earth, and subdue it.[109] Many times same-sex couples want to adopt in order to share in the experience of family. The only problem with this is that if their mindset and behavioral pattern were implemented fully throughout the earth prior to their being born, they would have never had the opportunity to be born.

Stop and think about that for a moment. Those who champion same-sex marriage and fight for the right to have love according to their own desires wouldn't be here to take such a stance if someone before them thought differently and lived out something opposite of what they currently believe. And to think that the experience of family would want to be shared in a compromised way is not right. It isn't right because it is marring God's original intentions. It is not just the *what* that is most important, but the *way* also; they must be in harmony.

The issue doesn't just stop with same-sex marriage. If you open up the box by completely destroying God's guiding definition, then there is no way to determine how devastating things can get. It's like dropping a

---

[109] Gen 1:28, NASB

huge stone into a body of water. You don't really know how far and wide the ripple effect of such an act will go.

It's the same with attempting to remove God's definition of love and marriage. If it isn't between a man and woman, then why not between a man and man, or a woman and a woman? But it doesn't stop there. Why not between multiple men, or multiple women? Or, why not between a man and an animal? Or, why not between an older man and a much younger man, like a minor?

There are just so many bizarre equations and outcomes that this produces. And that's why it's best that we surrender to God's ways, because they haven't been implemented to punish us but rather to protect us.

> **It's best that we surrender to God's ways, because they haven't been implemented to punish us but rather to protect us.**

The glamorization of sexual content over time has created many widespread issues. People's hearts, relationships, and marriages are being damaged through the perceived temporary enjoyment of pornographic content that is readily available. Something that lies and promises to satisfy immediately is wreaking havoc in a long-term sense.

Hollywood's marketing and many other companies that have joined in the belief that "sex sells" seek to benefit monetarily from promoting something on a big screen that reaps destruction in our hearts morally. Sex trafficking, issues of rape, prostitution, and even pedophilia, are all spawns from the glamorization of sex in our culture.

Something that seemed and felt harmless in its beginning stages has completely spiraled out of control. But this is the point—it felt right in the beginning. Something that may feel right produces many other issues in the world that are not right.

Racism, abortion, same-sex marriage, and the sex and pornographic industry would have to be dealt with when the powers of the air were properly dealt with in our hearts as a people and as a nation. Many more issues need to be dealt with. The mentioning of these is just to provide a beginning point for things that are glaringly obvious.

The influence of the powers of the air that are currently working in the hearts of people, when exposed and conquered, would bring a bright, shining light of God's heart and a proper alignment with His ways in our lives.

Real breakthrough would have to look like the removal of the influence of the powers of the air in the hearts and lives of people on the ground. The removal of such influence would automatically create a shift in culture. The removal of said influence in the lives of people would bring about dramatic and dynamic change in the way we approach life and one another. This is the breakthrough that is needed most. This is the breakthrough we must contend for through the posturing of our lives in fasting and prayer.

We can see churches full and meetings going nightly, but if they are full of people that have racism, bitterness, envy, malice, and more in their hearts, then we are not seeing the fullest measure of breakthrough that is needed. We can pack stadiums with people that are wild and exuberant in their dancing and declaration, but if they embrace mindsets that are hostile to God's ways and enjoy practices in their life that are influenced demonically, then we are not yet experiencing the greatest measure of real breakthrough that we seek.

We have to stop satisfying ourselves with the shallow and plastic goals that meet needs that we determine are immediate.

And this is the whole point—we have to stop satisfying ourselves with the shallow and plastic goals that meet needs that we determine are immediate, while they don't satisfy desires that God has that are ultimate. We need a fresh outpouring of God's Spirit. We need a real shaking of our hearts. We need to confront and deal with the issues that are real and the influence in our lives that holds up and keeps alive things that God wants to tear down and kill.

Oh God, would You grip the hearts of Your people and bring them to their faces before You in humility? Would You help us to rend our hearts and not just our garments? The days of professional and popularity Christianity must be cast off in order for an authentic and powerful people to arise.

We must rid from our hearts all of what seeks to infiltrate and lead us astray.

We are not truly powerful until and unless we are completely free from the influence of the powers of the air. We must rid from our hearts all of what seeks to infiltrate and lead us astray. It doesn't happen in a day, but neither did any of what we have discussed in this chapter thus far. Help us, Lord!

CHAPTER 10

WISDOM FROM ABOVE

"For My thoughts are not your thoughts, neither are your ways My ways."[110]

Our nation is the most divided that it has ever been. There is more hostility between people groups than we have ever faced. It is men vs. women, black vs. white, straight vs. LGBTQ, civilian vs. law enforcement, political party vs. political party, denomination vs. denomination, old vs. young, state vs. state, North vs. South, and on and on the list continues to go.

With so much swirling hostility, categorization, and division we have to dig a little deeper than the

---

[110] Isa 55:8, BSB

surface level conflict to identify the real source for what is fueling all of what is being experienced. The powers of the air are attempting to divide us so that they can destroy us. And please don't think for a moment that this is something that is only prevalent for unbelievers. The heat of these issues is just as real and can be felt just as strongly in the life of the Church, meaning those who claim a love for and allegiance to Jesus.

How do you even begin to approach all of the hostility? How do you attempt to successfully pray through everything that is happening around you? It really takes a greater wisdom. It really takes a higher perspective. Many times, the immediate solutions we believe will bring about a proper resolve to the issues and complexities of circumstances being experienced simply fall short in a long-term sense of being a real solution and producing lasting change. In many instances we simply apply bandages to severe wounds and hope to hide them so that the attention they have been gaining may be diverted.

The media plays an integral role in our day in the way that information gets distributed at large. The media does a great job at controlling the narrative. The media has a unique ability to drive people's attention to whatever issue, situation, or thing it wants to, by way of creating a buzz of attention in the direction of its desire.

From all of the various news outlets, to social media, to other independent media sources, there is a tug-of-war for who will determine the story line for what people are experiencing. And, if we are not careful and prayerful, we end up getting completely dragged around in the middle of the hysteria like a roller coaster at a theme park.

The media buckles us in by way of our attention, and then depending on if they want people to feel up or down, they provide information and supposed insights to pull in the direction that they want everyone else to go; it's an agenda.

It is important that we recognize the influence and the agenda that the media has and the influential role it takes in shaping our hearts and minds. We are not to be given over wholeheartedly to what the media communicates to us and allow that to be the source of our motivation and content in prayer.

It is critical to our success in prayer, and our posture in how we directly interact with God, others around us, and the issues at large in our time, that we sift our hearts of the role that the media plays and that we are not among those who are drowning in the deep end of the agenda that they are driving. It happens very easily, and many have become so intertwined in it that they have completely lost sight of it altogether and become overtaken.

Our hearts should be filled with what we hear and see in the place of God's council. The media alone is not our source for how to pray, or what to pray. If you receive insight and information as to what you allow to form the content of your prayer life through major news outlets or social media, you are missing the mark. You are not to turn your face to the media for insight; you are to turn your face to God.

Our hearts should be filled with what we hear and see in the place of God's council.

We are a people that have access to the mind of Christ. We are a people filled with the Holy Spirit. We are a people that have access into God's secret council. God's counsel is to be the dominant influence in our hearts and in our lives.

In days filled with so much confusion, counterviewpoints as to what is actually happening, and diverse opinions for the best way to help us move forward, it is key that we dial into the secret place for what is on God's heart and allow that to form our hearts as we set ourselves to fast and pray.

There is a place in the Old Testament where we can gain great insight into how to posture our lives for success in prayer, and it is found in the life of a prophet named Habakkuk. When you open up the book of Habakkuk you find a man that is processing in his heart all that is happening in his day. There is great devastation. The issues that Habakkuk sees are producing conflict in his heart because he is trying to reconcile what he sees against how good he knows God to be.

Habakkuk makes the statement in the opening chapter, "How long, O LORD, must I call for help? But you do not listen! 'Violence is everywhere!' I cry, but you do not come to save. Must I forever see these evil deeds? Why must I watch all this misery? Wherever I look, I see destruction and violence. I am surrounded by people who love to argue and fight. The law has become paralyzed, and there is no justice in the courts. The wicked far outnumber the righteous, so that justice is being perverted."[111]

You are not to turn your face to the media for insight; you are to turn your face to God.

It sounds as if Habakkuk is alive in our time and describing the situation unfolding in our day. He is a man experiencing hardship. He is alive in a time where his experience is producing confusion in his heart as to how everything that is happening is going to be resolved. How could God come and work wonders in the midst of such grave corruption?

---

[111] Hab 1:2-4, NLT

His heart is burdened by what he is seeing. He is overwhelmed by the conclusions he is drawing as he is searching round about and gathering the evidence. Even though he knows that God is good, things don't look good.

When God involves Himself in a situation everything must yield and bend to His influence and His desires.

If we aren't careful, after surveying the land it is easy to fall into the trap. We look around and deduce that things don't look good. Compromise is celebrated and championed by many. Justice is falling apart and the wicked are thriving. Perversion runs rampant and the speed of it is wildly accelerating.

Habakkuk is identifying the facts. There is nothing wrong with gathering the facts. We aren't weirdos that deny the facts. Facts are facts, and they do matter. However, as much as they matter, they alone are not all that there is to a matter. All of the facts that we gather absolutely fall subject to God. When God involves Himself in a situation everything must yield and bend to His influence and His desires. Habakkuk is about to realize just how true this is. Let's continue.

Habakkuk does something amazing, and we will use his actions to find a great point of encouragement. Habakkuk says these words in the beginning of the second chapter, "I will climb up my watchtower and stand at my guardpost. There I will wait to see what the LORD says and how he will answer my complaint."[112]

This is so amazing! I know that may seem a little premature because I haven't yet communicated why I think it is so amazing, so we should probably do that. Let's take a look at what Habakkuk says piece by piece, because it really is so good.

Habakkuk says I will climb up to my watchtower. Habakkuk is initiating a climb to a higher place. There is something really special about coming up to a higher place. Sometimes with all that we are facing and the things that currently surround us in life on the ground, what's most necessary is not a direct engaging of those things with our own perceived wisdom, but our climbing up to a higher place.

With all that we are facing in life on the ground, what's most necessary is climbing up to a higher place.

David, in the Psalms, writes these beautiful words, "From the end of the earth I will cry to You, when my heart is overwhelmed; Lead me to the rock that is higher than I."[113] We must fully realize in our hearts that there is a higher place

---

[112] Hab 2:1, NLT
[113] Ps 61:2, NKJV

than I. There is a place and a person that is greater than the I in our life, and it is God Himself.

As long as we believe that we are the greatest source of wisdom for ourselves we will never be awakened to the need that we have to climb up to a higher place. As long as we believe that we can muscle out an outcome or provide a solution for ourselves with all of the resources at our disposal, we will never find it necessary to respond to the still, small voice within our hearts that whispers, *Come up higher.*

Climbing to a higher place positions us to see things from a higher vantage point, from God's perspective.

Climbing to a higher place positions us to see things from a higher vantage point, from God's perspective. It is necessary that we understand how important it is to rise above all of the warfare that happens on the ground level of life. The continual warfare and fighting that happens on the ground easily forms the way that we see and directly impacts how we process and pray through what we are going through.

The entanglements found on the ground become a great deterrent from gaining a proper perspective to process and pray effectively. Effectiveness in processing our life and praying through issues effectively require coming up to a higher place.

John, on the Isle of Patmos, gives an account of an encounter that he had with the Lord, "After this I looked, and there before me was a door standing open in heaven. And the voice I had first heard speaking to me like a trumpet said, 'Come up here, and I will show you what must take place after this.' "[114]

Much like Habakkuk, John had to come up so that he could see what was to come. He had to come up so that God could show him what would've been difficult for him to see because of where he was standing. John had to get to a higher place in order for him to see clearly and receive revelatory insight pertaining to things that were to happen.

> **Getting up higher allows us to be free from the pressure of what we are currently experiencing so that we can see what God sees.**

This is the whole point. Getting up higher allows us to be free from the pressure of what we are currently experiencing so that we can see what God sees.

We see things in part. And in large part we are directly influenced by situations that we don't have all of the information about. So, with partial information we innocently pray our way through scenarios. However, our time in prayer should not only be

---

[114] Rev 4:1, NIV

informed by what we feel our situations are telling us. Using that method, we then lift our voices to God based on what we think is happening and what we believe would be the best outcomes. This is incomplete, at best.

We receive our instructions for intercession from up above.

Next, Habakkuk says that he is going to wait to see what it is that God will say. Here is where we find our strategy on how to approach our life and the situations we go through in prayer. We are not limited to only our opinion in prayer. Just as Habakkuk made a determination in his heart to wait and see what God would say, we too can resolve in our own hearts to do the same.

We receive our instructions for intercession from up above. We don't just have to pray what we feel; we can pray what God says. And we should be praying what God says, despite how we may feel.

It is important that we wait with the Lord in prayer. All of the urgencies, the instant demands, and the pressures that are applied to our hearts in life can and must be laid down at the feet of Jesus in prayer. Jesus is at rest. He is not anxious. He is not bent out of shape trying to figure out how He is going to bring needed corrections or implement solutions into your life or the earth.

In prayer we can come to Him with all of our burdens, lay them down, and wait with Him. Waiting has the power to disarm all of what is in our hearts that make us feel like we need to always have an immediate solution, answer, or strategy for things. Waiting is beautiful because it sifts the heart of what cannot wait and feels like it should move on without God.

Waiting is a key that opens up the door to revelation. Habakkuk determined to wait because he knew that he would see what God would say. Waiting is never in vain. For those who determine to wait upon the Lord, He never disappoints.

Habakkuk understood that in his waiting, he would see and hear. God is revelatory in nature. He just can't help it; it is who He is. When we draw near to Him, revelation flows out of Him. Just like Jeremiah prophesied that there was hearing and seeing in the secret counsel of the Lord,[115] we too have the privilege to see and to hear when we draw near to God.

For those who determine to wait upon the Lord, He never disappoints.

Habakkuk needed to see what God would say so it could break the hold off of his heart that was influenced by what he was only seeing. Until you see

---

[115] Jer 23:18, NASB

what God is saying, you are left up to your own inter-pretation of things, and this can be very limited and dangerous.

Revelation opens up our understanding so we can perceive what God is doing. God is not like us; His ways are not our ways, and His thoughts are not our thoughts. It is necessary for us to see what He is saying so our efforts in prayer can be in alignment with His will.

It is necessary for us to see what He is saying so our efforts in prayer can be in alignment with His will.

Too many times it is so easy to get wrapped up in our own agendas in prayer and think that because we attach God's name to it that it is exactly what He desires. Rather than praying what we desire and constantly asking God to bless our desires, it makes more sense to wait for revelation of what He desires and then join in agreement to what He already wants to do.

If you remain diligent to pray what you know God has revealed, then you will eventually see what you know it is that God has said. God will show you something by His Spirit and then challenge you to pray about it even when it may seem like a complete impossibility. You must be gripped with the sound of the abundance of rain on the inside and then go after it in prayer until the cloud the size of the man's hand begins to form.[116]

Being called up into a higher place is not just about being informed; it is also about becoming burdened. Too many want revelation, but they don't want God's burden. God intends for you to be different when you come back down because of all that He has revealed to you.

He is not just another Twitter comment or meme that you scroll across that can be easily dismissed. Oh no, God is looking for faithful friends that will partner with Him for what is on His heart. This is why He lets you in. He lets you in to what is on His heart so you can join Him in prayer for what He longs for.

> **God is looking for faithful friends that will partner with Him for what is on His heart.**

It will take great diligence to consistently pray what God has revealed. Many times, what God has revealed to you will be directly tested by what you are experiencing. This is the point. God unleashes revelation into your heart and then puts you on the ground in the middle of the chaos and says, "Now, pray it out! Pray it into existence. Release the word of the Lord and

---

[116] 1 Kings 18:44, NASB

watch everything about what you think is happening begin to shift!"

All impossibilities bow to Jesus. No darkness can remain when the light of the world breaks forth. All resistance loses its power when God begins to work. The word may test you for a season, and it may even put you in shackles in others, like Joseph,[117] but a word from the Lord cannot be denied!

All impossibilities bow to Jesus.

Not dialing in to the right influence, that being God's voice, will frustrate your efforts in prayer. Revelation should give you your instructions and marching orders for prayer and intercession. There is too much swaying and shifting with things that are given attention in a cultural sense. There are too many hot-topic or hot-button items that are flash-in-the-pan agendas depending on what is currently being circulated. But this is not our place in prayer, to be dragged around by whatever the newest or hottest subject matter is that is swirling round about.

We are to be grounded in God. We are to be steadfast and in alignment with His voice above all things. Even when you pray about immediate things, it should be from an ultimate and eternal perspective.

---

[117] Ps 105:17-19, NASB

In doing so, this will at times, lead you to pray things that sound completely absurd and may even cause you to seem delusional and uninformed, but that's okay. Be faithful with revelation. Revelation gives you the bull's-eye for God's desires.

Habakkuk understood that if he only looked at what he saw happening on the ground it would be a perpetual breeding ground for frustration and potential disappointment. But by climbing up to a higher place and waiting to receive revelatory insights from the Lord, his heart could be strengthened by God's perspective and His desires.

Don't abandon your place on the watchtower because what you heard hasn't come to pass as fast as you would've liked or thought.

The word of the Lord clears the air in our hearts. The word of the Lord minimizes the fog so we can be finely tuned to the real issues at hand that require our attention in prayer and not just all of the surface-level stuff that consumes the majority of our focus.

God has a plan; He has a will. God is a mastermind and an architect. Throughout all of history as we know it He has been building His desires into our timeline in order to arrive at the destination that He has already determined. Along the way we have the privilege and joy to join Him in praying for His Kingdom to come and His will to be done.

Don't abandon your place on the watchtower because what you heard hasn't come to pass as fast as you would've liked or thought. Too many decide to climb down, abandoning their place of hearing and seeing, because of disappointment with God's timetable. Don't be fooled into forfeiting your place of contending because things haven't material-ized as fast as you would've preferred. Just because you haven't seen it yet doesn't make God out to be a liar. Keep going for it.

Allow your burden to be formed in the secret place.

Elijah prayed six times and saw absolutely nothing, but he kept at it because he knew what God was saying. There was a stirring alive on the inside of him that wouldn't be denied by the material evidence around him that could have easily persuaded him to just quit. He kept at it, and on the seventh time the cloud became visible.

We must become a people willing to keep pressing in the place of prayer because we have become over-come with God's desires. Do not turn away from what you have seen and heard in the secret place. Keep praying it until you see it form in a public place.

Allow your burden to be formed in the secret place. Our real wisdom comes from above. The man who is truly wise is the one who is moved by what he knows God has said. Take all of your emotions and your ambitions to God and let Him sift through them and infuse them with divine fire.

Find your place in the secret place and join the Lord in prayer and intercession for hearts, homes, cities, regions, your nation, and the nations of the earth. You don't need a microphone to pray. You don't need a platform to join God in the secret place. You don't need any lights, camera, or action to be a faithful friend of the Lord and tarry with Him in the place of prayer.

Be willing to lay down any ideas or thoughts that don't align with what you know is on His heart.

Stop settling for worldly wisdom in prayer. Contend for God's perspective and His wisdom in prayer. Allow Him to be God in all of your processing and praying and be willing to lay down any ideas or thoughts that don't align with what you know is on His heart.

May you, like Habakkuk, make the decision to not remain down below. May you respond to the tug upon your heart to come up to a higher place. In the place of waiting on the Lord, may you see and hear afresh. May your heart become enlightened by the Spirit as to things that are to come. May the Lord fill your heart with a fresh zeal that empowers you in the secret place to cry out for what you know God is saying.

Contend for diligence in praying what you see and hear from the Lord so you can see what you know God is saying and revealing. It is time. There is much that depends on His faithful ones giving themselves in fasting and prayer to break open the fullness of His desires into the earth. I pray that you would become a part of that company, a faithful friend.

CHAPTER 11

DREAMS AND VISIONS

"And it shall come to pass afterward that I will pour out My Spirit on all flesh; Your sons and daughters shall prophesy, Your old men shall dream dreams, Your young men shall see visions."[118]

One of the simple and profound ways that God speaks to us is through dreams and visions. The Bible says that in the days of the outpouring of God's Spirit upon all flesh, one of the primary means of communication from God to humanity will be through the vehicle of dreams and visions.

---

[118] Joel 2:28; NKJV

In the days that we are living in, being filled with the Holy Spirit as believers in Jesus, we are privileged to be a people who are dreamers and visionaries. If you have been filled with the Holy Spirit you are a dreamer and a visionary. It is not as if to think that you could possess the Spirit, or better put—be possessed by the Spirit, and then decide to not check the box on the options list that would include dreams and visions in your life.

If you have been filled with the Holy Spirit you are a dreamer and a visionary.

As one that is filled with God's Spirit, you are a dreamer and a visionary. Now, with that said, that doesn't equally mean that you are doing the best job at cultivating this powerful reality in your life. But one thing that is for certain is that where the Spirit of the Lord is there are dreams and visions. God is a visionary. Your life, being filled with God, can be greatly impacted by the potent potential of dreams and visions.

One dream can change your entire life. Yes, you read that correctly. Going to sleep at night should produce a sense of awe and wonder. You never know which night will be the night that your sleep gets infused with revelation.

One of my favorite verses pertaining to dreams is found in Psalms chapter 16. David writes, "I will bless the LORD who has given me counsel; My heart also instructs me in the night seasons."[119]

Laying down and closing your eyes to rest for the night could be the very thing that propels you into the God-dream that changes everything about your life. One dream can change the trajectory. One dream can change the speed. One dream can change it all. It's important that we do not casually choose to ignore, as David described it, the night season. As people filled with God's Spirit, we must be open to the instruction that God may send us in the night.

As people filled with God's Spirit, we must be open to the instruction that God may send us in the night.

There have been many dreamers that God led in powerful ways through instruction that found its way to them in the night season. Consider Joseph who has the dream about his call and destiny in God.[120] Now, just because he saw something in a dream doesn't also mean that he handled it the best way that he could have.

---

[119] Ps 16:7; NKJV
[120] Gen 37:5, NASB

The point is that there was something in Joseph that recognized that God would not only speak and reveal His mysteries in dreams, but that God would also be able to speak to him personally. Joseph understood very well that God was investing His desires into his life through a dream. This was personal between God and Joseph, and Joseph was able to discern it.

Joseph is having dreams in the beginning of his life and later on he is interpreting the dreams of others. It's not enough to just have the experience, or to know that you had the dream. We also want and need the corresponding understanding or interpretation to the dream that God has deposited into our lives.

Many people feel paralyzed because they have experiences that go without explanations. This is not the way that God intends it. He doesn't want you to be stuck in neutral because you aren't able to discern what His intentions are through what He is saying or revealing. We must fast and pray for insight, understanding, and interpretation—just like Daniel did![121]

Daniel is another one that God led through the night. If you remember the story, Daniel and his friends are on the verge of losing their lives alongside of all the other wise men in Nebuchadnezzar's kingdom. They are in danger because the king has had

---

[121] Dan 10:2-3, NASB

a dream and makes a demand that seems wildly absurd and completely unrealistic to fulfill. Nebuchadnezzar wants someone to tell him his dream and then give him the interpretation!

All of the wise men are aware that no such request has ever been made and they think that the king has gone mad. However, when word gets to Daniel about what is happening, he has a very peculiar solution to the situation.

I have learned that sometimes the most spiritual thing you can do is go to sleep.

He gathers with his friends, Shadrach, Meshach, and Abednego, and they pray and ask God for mercy concerning the mystery. The Bible says they all went to sleep, and in the place of sleeping God reveals the mystery to Daniel in a night vision.[122] I have learned that sometimes the most spiritual thing you can do is go to sleep.

Daniel awakens and is overjoyed to realize that God has answered their hearts' cry and provided them with the much-needed insight to give the king what he requested, which also helps to deliver them from death. God told Daniel what the dream was that Nebuchadnezzar had and also the needed interpretation for its meaning. Wow, praise God!

---

[122] Dan 2:19, NASB

Joseph is a man that God led powerfully through a difficult moment by dreams. Joseph is engaged to Mary. However, Mary all of a sudden ends up pregnant and Joseph knows he is not the father. Now, let's pump the brakes for just a moment. I can understand how this situation would produce a little bit of trouble for any man that is set to be married. Let's not be too quick to be critical of Joseph.

The Bible describes Joseph as an upright and godly man, a man of character. He is set to dismiss Mary at night and end the engagement process because he doesn't want to shame her and produce any further complications for either of them. And on the night before he plans to do what he thinks is best, God intervenes and sends him a dream.

"But after he had considered these things, an angel of the Lord appeared to him in a dream, saying, 'Joseph, son of David, don't be afraid to take Mary as your wife, because what has been conceived in her is from the Holy Spirit. She will give birth to a son, and you are to name him Jesus, because He will save his people from their sins.' "[123]

Right when Joseph is getting ready to make a terrible mistake God is gracious and sends him a dream. Joseph can't really see that God is directly

---

[123] Matt 1:20-21, CSB

involved in what seems to be disrupting all of the plans he thought he had in place. A dream from God is what corrects Joseph's perspective. A dream is what realigns Joseph's heart to and with what God is doing. A dream is what God uses to fuel Joseph's heart with the much-needed fortitude to stand into and against all of the adversity that would soon unfold for him and his new family because of the way that God was working things out for them.

Don't underestimate the powerful role that a single dream from God can play in your life, call, and destiny.

Dreams are incredibly powerful. Don't underestimate the powerful role that a single dream from God can play in your life, call, and destiny.

Much of my life doesn't make a lot of sense if you remove the place of God's leadership and influence found in dreams. In fact, if you were to completely remove the dreams that have helped to shape my life and purpose in God I honestly don't know where I would be right now. God's leading through the night season has been an integral part of life and mission for my family and me.

We are not just dreamers, but we lean heavily upon God's promise that in these last days there would be dreams and visions filled with divine communication.

And this is the important point. It isn't just random dreams that we want, but it is God dreams.

Too many dreams are the byproduct of eating something before bed, watching a particular movie or show, or just a fleshly projection of our own desires into the place of our dreams. I say divine communication because not every dream is from the Lord—we will leave this subject for another book at another time.

My wife and I, and our kids now, have given our lives to fasting and praying to see revival. We burn to see revival in our hearts and in our home. We burn to see revival, a great and mighty outpouring of God's Spirit and an awakening, in our nation and the nations of the earth. We know that the Lord invited us into this life posture of fasting and praying to see this realized many years ago, and we have been going for it the best that we have known how. Not résumé building; Jesus loving. Not for the applause of some crowd, but for the smile of the One over the obedience of our lives.

In our pursuit and posture in life, God has many times given us insight on what and how to pray through dreams. This has played a significant role in how we have continued to posture our lives in fasting, praying, and contending to see revival break forth.

Now that we have briefly created a foundational place for the necessity of dreams and visions and the important role that God desires for them to play in how we walk out our life, I want to share a dream that I had a few years ago.

I was on an extended fast and had a dream that falls right into all that we are discussing here. I was confronted in a dream by what I knew was a principality. In much time fasting and praying about this encounter in the night I feel the Lord has graciously granted certain insights that have shaped the way we continue to fast and pray about our nation and the complete deconstruction of demonic influence that lingers and seeks to govern in specific ways.

Dream for the USA

I came into the dream and was standing in a parking lot on the edge of an enormous field. There were a lot of individuals there, but I knew that no one was there together; they were all there individually. There was great anticipation amongst the crowd. Everyone was waiting for something to happen and that is why they had all taken their individual places. I was looking around at all that was happening, but I didn't know why I was there.

I turned my attention back to the field. Out in the distance a being appeared. It had the form of a person and was clothed from head to toe in all black with a long cloak and a hood. As it drew closer, I could see that this being didn't have a male or female makeup.

Its face was smoky and glossed over and I knew that what I was looking at was a principality. I knew that the principality was a grand wizard—I didn't know what a grand wizard was. I had to google the term when I woke up and went to prayer.

As it kept coming closer to where we were all standing, the wizard was chanting in what I knew to be a demonic tongue, summoning strength from a dark place. The wizard was circling roundabout in the field and as the chanting grew louder the atmosphere shifted. There were dark, swirling clouds and loud thunder. The more chanting that happened the more the atmosphere changed and responded. I was trying to figure out why I was there, and also why no one else seemed to be moved by what they saw taking place out in the field.

Just then, the crowd split, making room for a very luxurious vehicle that had arrived. By the appearance of the vehicle I knew it had to be very expensive. The door to the back of the vehicle opened and a dark-skinned black gentleman stepped out. I knew that his name was Zeus. He was a large man. The reference for him in the dream was "the bodybuilder." The bodybuilder was dressed to impress; he had the look, the feel, the vibe. He was dressed to the nines, as they used to say.

He had a very developed physique. He flexed and appealed to the crowd that created a space for him.

The crowd erupted with applause, almost as if this is who or what they had been waiting for. The bodybuilder turned his attention from the crowd towards the field and walked towards the wizard.

The wizard and the bodybuilder began to face off. They started circling one another. At this point the wizard was increasing in volume with his demonic chanting. After a few moments I realized that this was not going to be a physical fight, but that this was a spiritual battle with very serious implications.

The bodybuilder stood in confidence against the wizard and at the top of his voice shouted three times, "Jesus Christ! Jesus Christ! Jesus Christ!"

To my utter amazement the wizard didn't seem fazed. He stopped for a moment, looked intently into the face of the bodybuilder, and said, "You think that is all that it takes? What will you do about these weapons, the weapons of: *Beauty, Vanity, Materialism,* and *Narcissism*? What will you do with these?"

At this, the bodybuilder's face changed, his countenance lowered, and I could tell that his confidence was shattered. He hung his head low, his body hunched over, and he took slow steps backwards.

It was at this moment that I backed away, trying to find a way to leave the scene, when a small black boy ran over to me. I looked at him and said, "Can you tell me where we are? I need to know what county we are in." He didn't say a word. I said, "Never mind, I have my cellphone on me." I pulled my cellphone out of my front right pocket and opened up an app like Google Maps. I did a pin drop and it blew up really big on the screen with the numbers of the area code to where we were; the area code was 631.

I turned to try and leave, and the young boy tugged at my shirt. I turned to look at him and he said to me, "Where are you going?" I responded, "I'm trying to get out of here!" He looked at me very gently, not seeming to be stirred by all of the hysteria of what was happening or my desire to leave, and said, "You don't understand, we need you here…"

This is when I was awakened.

Coming out of this dream I was greatly shaken. I didn't understand many of the details, but I was gripped with a sense of the gravity of the dream and the important place that I felt it played in and for what the Lord desires to do in the United States.

This is not to be exclusive to a particular nation, but rather to use what is spoken about as a means to create a platform in your heart for God to speak to you and encounter you in similar fashion as you posture your life in fasting and prayer to see breakthrough in your city and nation. I knew that God was speaking, and that it would also take fasting and prayer for the insights and interpretation to unfold. And that is exactly what I did; I began to fast and pray.

Any attack on unity is an assault on God's authority.

Let's look at some of the details of the dream and expound on them piece by piece. First, let me say that I believe that it is a dream that carries national implications and instructions. I believe with all of my heart that God has revealed insight into how we as a nation can experience true and lasting breakthrough, and not just some kind of seasonal move of the Spirit that is allowed to touch external things, yet never really cracks down deep to confront the key issues that are resisting the outpouring and awakening that many of our hearts are burning to see.

I was standing on the edge of a field and there were a lot of people there, but none of them were there together. Everyone was there as individuals. This reveals an issue with unity. Everyone was there holding down their own little space in the parking lot, but no two were actually there purposely together. The issue with unity is this—any attack on unity is an assault on God's authority. You can stand as a bunch of individual ones and all be speaking the same language and pursuing the same vision, but being a bunch of ones who are chasing the same thing is not the same as being one.

We are one body and we must contend for real unity by the Spirit. Paul's exhortation for us is to fight to preserve the unity of the Spirit in the bond of peace.[124] Paul recognized that it would take a fight to stay unified.

We are living in days where the Church is very divided. We are divided ethnically, socially, financially, politically, and denominationally. All of the divides, categories, and streams reveal a lack of true unity. You call it whatever you like; it is a lack of real unity.

Unity is not found in the adoption of a new language. Unity is not found in your ability to adapt to a specific mission and vision. Unity is not found because we all work for the same organization or regularly attend the same building. Those things are wonderful for what they are, but many times they are just plastic and hollow.

Real unity is only found in Jesus and the brokenness of our lives willing to prefer our brother as better

---

[124] Eph 4:3, NASB

than ourselves. Most of our conflicts and divides are issued out of a lack of desire to embrace the cross, go low, fast and pray for the wisdom of the Spirit, and come to true repentance and reconciliation. Yet, regardless of how difficult the biblical standard and prescription may be, it will never allow us an exemption. God's heart is God's heart, and His heart is that we be one, even as He is One.

Real unity is only found in Jesus and the brokenness of our lives willing to prefer our brother as better than ourselves.

Next, the principality that I encountered in the dream was a grand wizard. I honestly didn't know what this was. When I woke up and went to spend time in prayer, I had to google this term. I found out that it is an authoritative figure in the KKK. This was alarming to me; however, this continues to reveal the issue that race and racism are still alive and are still an issue that we must contend with in our nation.

Let's just say it this way, you cannot be a racist and be a Christian. You cannot claim to love Jesus and yet carry a hatred for another race in your heart. It doesn't matter to me where you are from or how you were raised. When you became born again all of what was attached to your old life and old man died, you became a new creation, and all things have become new.[125]

The bodybuilder who jumped out of the car was named Zeus. Zeus is Greek and means god. Also, Zeus, according to Greek religion, legends, and mythology, is the god of the sky, lightning, and thunder. Zeus is known to be the ruler of all the gods on Mount Olympus; he is the king of the gods.

We have to be careful that we don't fall in love with and worship our own man-made idea of who we want God to be.

Zeus, in the dream, is the representation of the god that we create in our own mind. He is the embodiment of all that man's wisdom and intellectual ability does to make our own version of God that we are willing to deal with, rather than embracing and loving Him as He is.

We attempt to make God more like us so we don't have to be confronted to become more like Him. We have to be careful that we don't fall in love with and worship our own man-made idea of who we want God to be.

The bodybuilder is an interesting figure in the dream. The bodybuilder had the luxurious vehicle. Cars can represent ministry in dreams. He had the

---

[125] 2 Cor 5:17, NASB

very expensive and flashy vehicle. He also had the personal look and the appeal. He had the right style that was currently trending or relevant to the desires of the crowd.

The crowd had created a space for him. It was almost as if the crowd had been waiting for someone like this to arrive, and gladly created a space for his car. The bodybuilder flexed and showboated for the oohs and aahs before heading out to confront the wizard. There is much to be said about all of this.

Our generation is caught up in who is going to be the next big thing. Who's going to arrive on the scene with the next high-producing, money-making, applause-generating kind of ministry? Our generation has a fixation with popularity and equates that with anointing, power, and stature in God. The two do not mean the same thing.

God doesn't determine stature in the Kingdom by how many subscribers you have on YouTube, followers you have on Instagram, or likes you have on Facebook or Twitter. Your stature isn't determined by how much applause you generate from the crowd. It's not your trendy look or new cool way of being relevant. People can make room for you

People can make room for you and approve of you, but this doesn't mean that God has authorized you.

and approve of you, but this doesn't mean that God has authorized you. Status with men and stature in God are not the same thing. Stature in God can create status with men, but status with men does not always mean that you have stature in God. The bodybuilder found out the hard way that these things are not what determine a powerful person in the Spirit.

The term bodybuilder in itself is really funny when considered in light of the details of the dream. The Church is referred to as the Body of Jesus. And a builder is one we would ascertain that has the unique gifting or ability to build, and to build well. This bodybuilder had a massive and well-put-together physique. The visual credentials of this builder would have brought you to the conclusion that he was one that understood the needed ingredients in building a big body. However, looks can be very deceiving.

The bodybuilder went out to face off with the wizard and realized that though he was able to build a big body physically, he didn't carry the needed authority in the realm of the Spirit to deal with the principality. This is where we don't always see what God sees. We think that because a church is really big that they must also carry big-time authority. Only God knows what we build and how we build. Regardless of what weight we may feel we carry, God is the one that determines our stature.

All of the outer façades and gimmicks that we know how to employ to develop prominence with people in an earthly way is not what God looks at. God told Samuel, "Don't judge by his appearance or height, for I have rejected him. The LORD doesn't see things the way that you see them. People judge by outward appearance, but the LORD looks at the heart."[126]

The bodybuilder shouted the name of Jesus three times and it didn't prove to phase the principality at all. In fact, the principality responded with something that was very startling, "You think that's all that it takes? What will you do about these weapons…?" We will get to the weapons in a moment.

I know it is very challenging theologically to think that the principality wouldn't just back down or vanish upon the name of Jesus coming off the lips of the bodybuilder, but let us not be so quick to come to our own conclusions. Remember the sons of Sceva in the book of Acts? They attempted to cast out the demon from the man who was possessed, and what happened? They said, "In the name of Jesus, whom Paul preaches… come out!" And then the evil spirits replied and said, "Wait, Jesus we know, and Paul we know, but who are you?" And then the men were severely beaten, bloodied, and stripped naked and embarrassed.[127]

---

126 1 Sam 16:7, NLT
127 Acts 19:13-16, NLT

When it comes to spiritual authority, it isn't the external mimicking of activities that matter most. The sons of Sceva used the name of Jesus in a manner they had seen Paul do, I am sure, only they didn't come away with the same result as Paul would. They were unknown in a demonic realm. The evil spirits didn't respect them, because they didn't have authority.

You will never be able to evict what you secretly entertain.

The wizard looked at the bodybuilder and asked what his strategy was to deal with the weapons that were wielded against him. Quick note here—the enemy always overplays his hand, and in most cases, he fires early. The principality said the weapons of warfare that were being used were: beauty, vanity, materialism, and narcissism.

What was the principality really saying? The principality was communicating that the bodybuilder wanted to come and give him an eviction notice from the territory that he occupied but couldn't yet find a way to evict his influence out of his own heart.

This is devastating to consider. The influence wielded against the bodybuilder was something that had been embraced. All of the weapons that the principality used to gain a place of authority were working, and the bodybuilder didn't have an answer for it. The name of Jesus came off of his lips, but the influence of the principality resided in his heart.

This is the truth of the matter: you will never be able to evict what you secretly entertain. Meaning, if you want to see it conquered publicly, you have to see it conquered privately. You must deal with it in your heart before you deal with it in the streets.

You may see measures of breakthrough, but you won't be able to break it wide open according to God's fullest and deepest desires. You cannot gain authority over what you have embraced. Public displays of power will always flow from private battles and victories.

The bodybuilder embraced all of the influence of the weapons in his own heart and lifestyle and the principality knew it. It shattered the confidence of the bodybuilder and he retreated. This should not be. We need authentic opposition to arise. We need those who have been powerfully changed and delivered by the power of God and are now ready to bring that same deliverance that they have tasted and seen in the privacy of their own lives to the public arena.

God looks for those who were broken and have now found their wholeness in Him and are ready to bring that to others.

God doesn't look for well-put-together images that are hollow and lack substance and authority. He looks for those who were broken and have now found their wholeness in Him and are ready to bring that to others. God is raising up a people of stature to demolish the strongholds of the enemy.

The area code 631 is for Babylon, NY. Yes, you just read that right. The city of Babylon is where the area code 631 is. There are many other things that could be said about this, but for now let's identify that God will use a variety of things that seem mysterious, but are also very practical at times, in order to communicate His points.

The place that this principality had set himself up in order to wield his influence against a nation was Babylon. Babylon is the city referenced in the book of Revelation, "She has become a dwelling place for demons, a haunt for every unclean spirit, a haunt for every unclean bird, a haunt for every unclean and detestable beast. For all nations have drunk the wine of the passion of her sexual immorality, and the kings of the earth have committed immorality with her, and the merchants of the earth have grown rich from the power of her luxurious living."[128]

Each of the weapons the principality revealed it was using to create an entry point for influence don't really seem like all that big of a deal at first glance. But

---

[128] Rev 18:1-3, ESV

let's take a moment and unpack each of these weapons and bring clarity on how devastating of a strategy this actually is.

It's important to notice how each of these weapons are weapons directly formed in and from the character of the enemy himself. The goal of the enemy's influence is to get us to become like him—operating in his likeness and not God's.

The goal of the enemy's influence is to get us to become like him—operating in his likeness and not God's.

Beauty can be defined this way: the quality present in a thing or a person that gives intense pleasure or deep satisfaction to the mind, whether arising from sensory manifestations, meaningful design or pattern, or something else.[129] It is things that are satisfying and appealing to our natural senses. No big deal, right? Wrong. Beauty challenges the way we satisfy our natural cravings. It speaks directly to what we do to satisfy the longing that our fleshly senses generate with us.

The natural senses deal with what you watch, what you hear or listen to, what you taste, what you touch, and what you smell. This becomes a really big deal when we consider all of what we are convinced to do

---

[129] Dictionary.com, https://www.dictionary.com/browse/beauty.

in our time of felt need in order to gratify the lustful desires that arise and rage within us.

The weapon of beauty is a direct confrontation with how you satisfy yourself. The things you watch that potentially bring you into bondage—Hollywood, sports entertainment, the pornographic and sex industry, the constant images that you scroll over and the pages that you follow, the channels on YouTube that you subscribe to, and the videos you may watch.

We were made to be satisfied on every level by Jesus.

It deals with what you taste and the addictive nature that resides in all of our fleshly capacities. Addiction to alcohol, drugs, and other substances is devilish because it causes us to crave something other than Jesus. It deals with how we consume food, and food bondages that are created through our uncrucified cravings.

Beauty deals with what we touch; the sexual urges that consume us which turn into masturbation, fornication, prostitution, sex trafficking, pedophilia, and many other sexual avenues that are entertained to satisfy this felt need. Beauty deals with the music we choose to listen to; the sounds and language that we absorb into our spirit. Beauty is an overall inspection of what and who we turn to in order to satisfy ourselves in our times of need. We were made to be satisfied on every level by Jesus. The issue of beauty must be considered and dealt with in our hearts on every level.

In Ezekiel we are given a prophetic description of the enemy, "You were the seal of perfection, full of wisdom and perfect in beauty. You were in Eden, the garden of God. Every kind of precious stone adorned you: ruby, topaz, diamond, beryl, onyx, and jasper, sapphire, turquoise, and emerald. Your mountings and settings were crafted in gold, prepared on the day of your creation. You were anointed as a guardian cherub, for I had ordained you. You were on the holy mountain of God; you walked among the fiery stones. From the day you were created you were blameless in your ways—until wickedness was found in you. By the vastness of your trade, you were filled with violence, and you sinned. So I drove you in disgrace from the mountain of God, and I banished you, O guardian cherub, from among the fiery stones. Your heart grew proud of your beauty; you corrupted your wisdom because of your splendor; so, I cast you to the earth; I made you a spectacle before kings."[130] The enemy's infatuation with himself corrupted his wisdom. His satisfaction with his own beauty became his demise.

Vanity is an excessive pride in one's appearance, qualities, abilities, or achievements. Vanity deals with

---

[130] Eze 28:12-17, BSB

our obsession with what we look like, how great we perceive ourselves to be, what we feel we are capable of, and all of the awards and applauses that our lives have generated. Vanity is linked to pride, power, and prestige. Vanity is being swallowed up in yourself. It is the embodiment of a self-absorbed life.

We must be reminded that it is the enemy that is spoken of through the prophet Isaiah this way, "But you said in your heart, 'I will ascend to heaven; I will raise my throne above the stars of God, And I will sit on the mount of assembly in the recess of the north. I will ascend above the heights of the clouds; I will make myself like the Most High.' "[131] The self-made, self-exalted, prideful one is the enemy, and this desire is one of the reasons that led to his being cast down out of the heavens.

It is not hard to identify the places where this may hit very hard in our culture. The flashy lights. The desire for fame and stardom. The absolute obsession with a specific look and feel that Hollywood, social media, and many other places tell us is what should be hotly pursued in order to be considered acceptable. The person who finds their value and identification with the world and others through their next accomplishment, that next applause, award, degree, or promotion.

---

[131] Isa 14:13-14, NASB

Vanity speaks to the unhealthy fitness industry. Vanity deals with the pride of life, man's desire to make himself great. I am not saying that all ambition and determination is wrong. I think you understand clearly the point that is being made here. The bondage is being consumed with yourself, the pursuit of yourself, and the continual need for celebration of yourself.

Materialism is one that is rather obvious because of the definition that I am sure we are all familiar with for the term. However, let's take a fresh look at the definition for materialism. Materialism is a preoccupation with or emphasis on material objects, comforts, and considerations, with a disinterest in or rejection of spiritual, intellectual, or cultural values.[132]

The familiarity usually gets had with the first part of the definition—the preoccupation with material objects. But, the second half of the definition is equally as meaningful. Materialism is an anchoring in this life, here and now. The money hungry that attempt to generate their value by their ability to generate great wealth and possessions. It is a posture in life that reflects a value on this life, in an immediate sense, with all of its things and stuff. It is the defining of our lives by the things that we have, or don't have. You can see how dangerous this becomes.

---

[132] Dictionary.com, https://www.dictionary.com/browse/materialism?s=t.

We are not to identify our lives and values by what we have. Remember the rich young ruler in Mark's gospel who was saddened by Jesus' invitation to follow Him because it came with severing himself from his things. The Bible actually says that he turned down Jesus' invitation and walked away saddened because he was one that had many possessions.[133] Another translation said he owned much property.[134] And yet another translation says he had great wealth.[135]

We must be able to have things and not have our things have us.

Our hearts and lives are not to be tethered to this world, for it is not our home. We must live in the world, but not be of the world. We must be able to have things and not have our things have us.

The bondage of our heart to a specific lifestyle, or status in life, is what is confronted here. Our ability to fully follow Jesus when the cost is separating from our stuff is the confrontation. It is the enemy who wanted to take his throne (a possession) and exalt it above God's position in his life.

And the last weapon mentioned was narcissism. Narcissism is an inordinate fascination with oneself;

---

[133] Mark 10:22, CSB
[134] Mark 10:22, NASB
[135] Mark 10:22, NIV

excessive self-love; vanity. The issue in our day is that we are constantly being told to just be ourselves, and that people should love us as we want to be. Just be you, because Jesus loves you. But what if the way that you love the idea of who you want to be is in direct opposition to who Jesus made you to be?

Jesus loves you enough to set you free from the love of yourself that creates a particular bondage to your own desires. Revelation gives us this powerful verse, "And they have conquered him by the blood of the Lamb and by the word of their testimony, for they loved not their own lives even unto death."[136] Another translation writes the last portion this way, "And they did not love their own lives so much that they were afraid to die."[137] It's the beginning of this verse that most times generates all of the applause and the amens.

Jesus loves you enough to set you free from the love of yourself that creates a particular bondage to your own desires.

It is the enemy that will not submit himself to God. The enemy is radically opposed to the idea of surrendering his life to God and yielding to His leadership. He was removed from the heavens for this very reason. Jesus said to Peter, "Get behind me, Satan! You are a

---

[136] Rev 12:11, ESV
[137] Rev 12:11, NLT

stumbling block to Me. For you do not have in mind the things of God, but the things of men."[138]

Jesus knew the voice of the enemy because He was familiar with the character of the enemy. Jesus was talking about laying his life down and the enemy was attempting to sway him. The enemy will stop at nothing in order to detour you from laying your life down to God.

The enemy will stop at nothing in order to detour you from laying your life down to God.

We understand the victory of the blood of Jesus and the word of our testimony over the enemy, and that should be celebrated, praise God! But, that reality is and should also produce a people that fully embody the second portion of the verse—we have lost the love of ourselves in the love of Jesus and we are not afraid or ashamed to pay the ultimate price for Him because He has paid it for us.

Most times we really do have a love for Jesus that is real and genuine. It is, however, just not greater than the love that we have for ourselves. We sing songs that declare our life doesn't belong to us and we are willing to go anywhere God says and do anything that God may want. But this is hotly contested in our hearts

---

[138] Matt 16:23, BSB

when the cost of our lives or who we think we are is at stake.

Self-preservation comes up with a lot of spiritually sounding wise arguments as to why paying a price for Jesus is not worth it. You may really love Jesus, but when you have to choose between the love you have for yourself and the love you have for Him, the choice always sides with self. The blood of the Lamb has the power to conquer self-love in our hearts, self-love that opposes a complete surrender, death, and burial in the love of God for us.

As you can see, from an outer and quick glance the weapons that the principality revealed didn't seem to carry that much weight to them. But as we have taken the needed time to lightly expound upon each one and the weightiness of them in our hearts and lives, it is a very serious matter.

The blood of the Lamb has the power to conquer self-love in our hearts, self-love that opposes a complete surrender.

We will never be able to evict what we personally entertain. If you embrace it privately you will struggle to oppose it publicly. This is not to say that you cannot masquerade around in a showman type of way. But I mean the carrying of real dynamic authority from the Lord to see breakthrough and bring real deliverance to people's hearts and lives.

We must contend with our own hearts and then set the captives free.

It is necessary to allow the Spirit to evaluate what is in our hearts. This is where fasting becomes crucial. Many times, we are just not aware of how deeply something is affecting us. It takes the Spirit to reveal the vices in our hearts and lives that have formed over time.

We will have to see breakthrough in the heart of the Church if we want the Church to be the agent to bring breakthrough to the nation.

I don't imagine that anyone wakes up every day and thinks, "Today seems like a good day to give in to the influence of powers and principalities!" I don't believe that at all. However, even if that isn't your intention, if you don't intentionally expose your heart to God and allow Him to speak into it constantly, it easily happens.

Fasting keeps the lights on so that nothing can hide in the dark corners. Fasting and prayer keeps the proper amount of exposure on our hearts before the Lord so that He has the freedom and necessary time and space to speak to things that we may not see.

Would you join me in praying for our nation? I would love to see these weapons dealt with in the heart of the Church. We will have to see breakthrough in the heart of the Church if we want the Church to be the agent to bring breakthrough to the nation.

I am believing God for a day when these weapons get crushed by the power of the Spirit and we see people's lives drastically shaken into freedom. These weapons wielded against us do not have to prosper. Will you take up the fight and contend in prayer for the tearing down and demolishing of these strongholds?

God looks for people to involve themselves in the fight and no longer casually sit by on the sidelines of history. You are here now. God put you here now. This is your watch, your generation. Enter into consecration with God, fast and pray, and let your life become a weapon in the hand of the Lord! It's time!

Enter into consecration with God, fast and pray, and let your life become a weapon in the hand of the Lord!

My intention is to reveal what has been revealed to me and to implore you on behalf of the Lord, it is time to rise up. Divine strategy is needed in this warfare. This is not left to the carnal and the self-proclaimed mighty.

God is faithful to reveal strategy in dreams. God is faithful to bring counsel in the night season. God is gracious enough to intervene with us in our lives in times when what we need most is intervention and activation. This is exactly what we will discuss in our next chapter.

May God awaken us to the powerful potential that we possess by His Spirit in our generation to turn the tide of history and see His dreams realized over our lives and the nations of the earth.

CHAPTER 12

INTERVENTION AND ACTIVATION

"Do not eat or drink for three days and nights. My servant girls and I will do the same. Then I will go in to see the king, even if it means I must die."[139]

We have already taken a glimpse into the life of Esther, so we won't spend much time here recreating the context. There is a part of Esther's life and call that all of us must contend with at some stage in our decision to walk with God.

---

[139] Est 4:16, CEV

Esther has been blessed in a tremendous way. She came from nothing and now has everything. Esther has believed, and she has received. There is so much that God has done in Esther's heart and life. She has a story that reveals God's goodness and ability to triumphantly lead us through seasons of tragic circumstances and make miraculous provisions so the fulfillment of His words and desires are accomplished. If there is anyone throughout the history of the Scriptures who has seen God do great things, it is Esther.

Esther has seen God do great things in her life, but that doesn't disqualify her from facing challenges in her future. Esther has seen miracles, but that also doesn't mean that she won't ever need one again.

There comes that special window of time in Esther's life when all of the Jews are to be killed. Esther is sitting in the palace when all of her people are scrambling in the streets. The Jews are in their homes fasting, praying, and crying out to God for their deliverance. Esther is sitting in luxury while her people are experiencing hostility.

Esther has been raised up to occupy the place that she is in. It is no doubt that God has put her into this position. Now Esther has to confront the hard, cold facts as to the real reason why God did all that He did to get her into the place that she currently occupies.

The report comes to Esther from her uncle, Mordecai. He gives it to her servant, Hathach, who delivers the letter that reveals all of the plans and purposes for her people, the Jews, to be exterminated. Mordecai also sends this request, "Show this to Esther and explain what it means. Ask her to go to the king and beg him to have pity on her people, the Jews!"[140]

When Esther receives the message from Mordecai, she evaluates the situation that is unfolding before her and sends a message to Mordecai in response. "She answered, 'Tell Mordecai there is a law about going in to see the king, and all his officials and his people know about this law. Anyone who goes in to see the king without being invited by him will be put to death. The only way that anyone can be saved is for the king to hold out the gold scepter to that person. And it's been thirty days since he has asked for me.' "[141]

After analyzing the situation at hand, Esther makes an informed decision. She understands that there is a very real situation affecting her people. She knows that there is a great urgency for something to happen in their favor or else things won't turn out well for them. But what she also understands is that what Mordecai is asking her to do comes with a very high price, in fact,

---

[140] Est 4:8, CEV
[141] Est 4:10-11, CEV

the ultimate price to pay—potentially the laying down of her life—and this consideration shakes her heart.

When she considers what her involvement in this situation could cost her, the only reasonable decision to make is to send back to Mordecai that everybody around understands the law, and everybody is aware of what happens to any and all who would choose to break that law. Esther is essentially saying, "There is a certain protocol here, Mordecai, and what you are asking of me would immediately jeopardize all of the other things that God is doing with me."

Esther's platform is a testimony of what God can and will do with those that love and trust Him.

In some ways I can understand the thought process and the conclusion that Esther comes to. She has gone through a lot to get where she is. God has done incredible things to deliver her from impossible beginnings and delivered her into an improbable outcome. Esther's platform that she now stands on is a testimony of what God can and will do with those that love and trust Him.

There is no doubt that Esther has in mind all that God has done. Part of the way that she is considering Mordecai's request is being filtered through what she thinks God is doing and what she believes God has in mind for where she finds herself. The only problem with this is that for as many times as we need to have our hearts washed afresh with this beautiful and challenging reminder—God isn't like us and He doesn't think like us. God isn't necessarily thinking about Esther's position the way that Esther is thinking about her position.

Esther has been put into a place that serves a great purpose. She just hasn't seen it all clearly yet the way that God sees it. Esther is weighing the cost and attempting to back down from the very moment that God has put her into position for.

The challenge and fire of the moment seems too hot for Esther to bring herself to grips with the possibility that God may not be interested in protecting her from what is unfolding. But maybe, just maybe, what is unfolding is one of the great reasons behind why God worked so hard to make sure that she was in the right place when it all went down.

You didn't put yourself where you are; God did it for you.

Esther's purpose is not to protect her platform. It is not her platform to protect. God put her where she is. At times, we must also be reminded of this beautiful truth. You didn't put yourself where you are; God did it for you. He found you. He touched your life. He raised you up. He made all of the connections and opened all of the doors. He provided. He made a way when there seemed to be no way.

There is nothing you have done in your own strength to make happen what has happened, so it is only right that there is nothing for you to feel protective about. Esther wants to protect herself from her purpose. But the painful fear of the cost involved clouds her mind and she isn't processing things the same way that God is.

Thank God for people that He strategically places in our lives in times of great need to put our perspective into proper alignment with His heart.

Mordecai doesn't just back down when he receives Esther's response; he sends one more message. He sent back this reply, "Do not imagine that you in the king's palace can escape any more than all the Jews. For if you remain silent at this time, relief and deliverance will arise for the Jews from another place and you and your father's house will perish. And who knows whether you have not attained royalty for such a time as this?"[142]

Thank God for people that He strategically places in our lives in times of great need to put our perspective into proper alignment with His heart. Esther may

---

[142] Est 4:13-14, NASB

not be able to clearly see what God intends to do, but Mordecai sees something that he isn't afraid to share with Esther. Mordecai has been set up by God to bring an intervention to Esther. You can almost hear it in the tone of his voice.

"Esther, wake up! You have been blinded by the way that you have been blessed. Esther, please, wake up! You are standing in the right place, but you are serving the wrong purpose. Esther, if you do not wake up to God's purpose for why He has you in the position that you are in, you are about to miss it; you are going to blow it, Esther.

The fear of harm, destruction, and death is a very powerful tool that forms our decisions in a very real way.

"You are about to miss out on the very reason that God has brought you into the position of stature. Esther, do not allow your enjoyment of where you are to cause you to miss out on why you are there. Esther, now is your moment; this is your time. Esther, you have to consider this and see it the way that God sees it. I know there is a great cost involved, but what if paying that price is your purpose?"

Self-preservation is a powerful motivation. The fear of harm, destruction, and death is a very powerful tool that forms our decisions in a very real way. None of us goes out on a day-to-day basis looking for ways to put ourselves directly in danger. I have a wife and children, and it is a joy for me to be with them. I don't think about doing things that would prevent me from coming home at the end of the day.

Self-preservation can be something that helps inform our hearts of the right decisions to make in different moments. This is what Esther must be shaken of. Her heart must face the real consideration that God's purpose could cost her the ultimate price, her life. Fear always attempts to influence our decisions. And, oftentimes, fear sounds a lot like wisdom to those who hold dear to self-preservation.

There are eternal purposes that are directly attached to the place that God has put you in life.

Now, please hear this clearly. We aren't talking about some wild Rambo complex where we are intentionally creating some situation that comes with a severe penalty attached to it just because. That is just strange. We are speaking of moments in life where our involvement in the purposes of God comes with a price, or a cost that must be counted. This is where Esther is; she is having to count the cost.

But thank God for a voice that shakes her free from a perspective that only takes into account the immediate reward. The immediate reward is that she can preserve her life from the pain and trouble of breaking the rules and speaking with the king. The immediate benefit is that she doesn't have to trouble the platform that God has given her. She can continue to enjoy all of what she enjoys because of where she has been placed.

Like Esther, we must not allow the enjoyment of where we are to be the very thing that prevents us from serving God's purposes with where we are. Mordecai says, "What if this is the very reason that God put you into the position that you are in?" We too must consider this question in light of things that are not just immediate, but ultimate and eternal.

There are ultimate implications attached to your platform. There are eternal purposes that are directly attached to the place that God has put you in life. Your position, and all that comes along with it, may be the very stage that God looks for history to be hinged upon. Like Esther, what will you do with your moment?

A self-preservation people bound by self-love will not be the type of people that spark revival in the earth.

The verse in Revelation is one that I would like to bring back to your attention. "And they did not love their lives so as to shy away from death."[143] We want to be a

---

people that are willing to give everything to God, even our lives if it calls for that.

A self-preservation people bound by self-love will not be the type of people that spark revival in the earth. That sounds strong, and I intend it to be so. Those who are afraid to give it all to Jesus, whether literally by the laying down of their own lives, or just in other measures when the cost of following Jesus fully will come with some sort of severe penalty, are not the catalytic people that will shake the earth.

If loving Him well costs me everything, there is nothing worth holding onto, not even my own life.

The people that will shake the earth are those that have looked deeply into the face of Jesus and found everything that their heart has ever desired and have come to the deliberate conclusion that He is worth everything. Therefore, if loving Him well costs me everything, there is nothing worth holding onto, not even my own life.

There are a people that God has formed throughout the history of the age, and is forming now, that have been so deeply overtaken by the love of Jesus that they couldn't possibly bow to the altar of fear because their life has already been sacrificially offered up to Him on the great altar of love. Perfect love casts out all fear.[144] It is Tertullian that is remembered for saying, "It is the blood of the martyrs that is the seed of the Church."[145]

Consider John the Baptist. John is put into prison because of his righteousness and his decision to deliver a word to the king that didn't sit well with him. John declares to Herod that his actions with his brother's wife are unlawful.[146] John delivered a word of conviction and he was put into prison.

I am sure John calculated the cost. I am sure John realized the severity of the price he would pay if he went forward with what God put in his heart to release. But the point is this; he went forward anyway. He wasn't trying to protect his ministry. He wasn't worried about all of those who could have rallied around him to offer their insights and wisdom.

There are so many voices. Can't you just hear them? "John, this really isn't the best move for you, at least not right now. We've been working hard for you to build your brand." "John, God is really using you right now, and if you do something silly like this it is going to directly jeopardize all that God has worked so hard to do with you and for you." "John, clearly you

---

144 1 John 4:18, NASB

145 Inspiringquotes.us, https://www.inspiringquotes.us/author/1938-tertullian.

146 Matt 14:4, NASB

aren't seeing things the way that God is. You should just remain silent right now because the people really need to hear you preach for another few years or even decades."

I am sure that something like this piled into John's heart prior to him lifting up his voice, but he lifted it anyway. In the face of persecution, he lifted it. In the face of a great price to be paid, he lifted his voice. Up against the thought of potentially losing his own life, John preached the truth!

We know that John's life is one that was conditioned by fasting and prayer. Jesus tells us that John came with fasting and prayer.[147] He was conditioned in the wilderness with God through the constant offering up of his own appetite. God developed John through a consistent brokenness experienced through fasting and prayer.

In great weakness and brokenness God develops strength and boldness.

Fasting has a way of bringing our lives into an induced weakness and brokenness that in many cases just cannot be experienced any other way. Brokenness before God is what prepared John to be broken of the thought to preserve himself for the world.

---

[147] Matt 11:18, NASB

In great weakness and brokenness God develops strength and boldness. John offered up his appetite and it is what prepared him to take that great stand in the day that would call him to offer up his head.

And this is what is so great about Esther's response to Mordecai. She sends back to him that they are to enter into a fast for the next three days and nights. At the conclusion of the fast she is planning to go in and speak with the king. It is at this point that she makes the declaration, "And if I perish, I perish."[148]

There is something about the way that the story is told that informs us that Esther realizes that a fast is necessary for her to consider the great cost of her life. There is a sense in the text that Esther knows that going to God in fasting and prayer will be a way to find His wisdom and favor, but also His boldness to lay down her life if that is what it costs her.

Does she want God to supernaturally intervene and make a way for national deliverance and victory? Absolutely. Is she certain that is what will happen if all of them fast and pray together? Absolutely not. But, has she determined in her heart that no matter what the outcome is for her, she will fast and pray, and God will strengthen her heart to rise up to the occasion and

---

[148] Est 4:16, CSB

join in to the purposes of God for this moment in her life even if she perishes? Absolutely!

Esther needed an intervention to activate her for God's purpose. And maybe you do too. Have you considered that what you have been working so hard to protect may be the very thing that God is asking you to give to Him for His purposes to be fulfilled? It may not be that you have to lay down your life in actuality. But it may be the idea of what your life and platform that God has given to you are supposed to be utilized for.

It could be your idea for the vision of your business that God is asking for. It could be your political plat- form. It could be the financial stature that you enjoy. It could be your kids that God has blessed you with and now you are fearful about fully releasing them over to the Lord and His call on their lives. It could be your spouse. It could be the direction of your church.

There are a million ways this could play out in your heart and life. These examples are only to provide a few ways of what it may look like for you as you process with God what the cost of fulfilling your purpose in Him may be due to where He has placed you.

The eyes of the Lord are searching for someone who will get in the game. There are too many burning with a desire to get involved that timidly stand on the sidelines and have a real disinterest in ruffling any feathers by jumping up off the bench.

Too many have abandoned their post for the enjoyment of this life and its immediate rewards. These things were never to be the premier things that we live for. Even in the midst of all of the complacency, God looks. God aggressively hunts down any and all that want their life to count in light of eternity. God sifts through the hearts of men and women with a jealousy to awaken hearts to His purposes.

God sifts through the hearts of men and women with a jealousy to awaken hearts to His purposes.

It is beautiful that fasting and praying helped Esther engage God's purposes. It is amazing that a life of fasting and praying prepared John the Baptist to fulfill God's desires. And what about you? I encourage you that a fasted life will help you to determine God's will. I encourage you that a fasted life will break the chains of self-love and the attractions of the world's rewards to freely and fully give God everything, no matter the cost.

Too many are intimidated by the penalty of righteousness. Too many bow down at the altar of fear. Too many are completely crippled by the world, its pressures, and the pain of rejection that come along with standing up and into God's purposes. Too many have chosen to die to their purpose in order to protect their platform.

But, may God put something in your heart, that like Esther, says, "I realize what God is doing in this hour, and if it costs me everything to fulfill my purpose, then so be it! I would rather die serving my purpose in God than die to my purpose attempting to protect my platform or position!"

It is time for you to be awakened and activated unto and into the purposes of God in your life and in your generation.

May your loving devotion and consecration to God be a dynamic, provocative element that causes the eruption of others around you to burn with fiery love. May God do something in you that shakes the world around you. It is time for you to be awakened and activated unto and into the purposes of God in your life and in your generation. May you be one that doesn't die sitting on the sidelines just critiquing how the game was unfolding. Get up! Get ahold of God! Get involved!

Give yourself to fasting and praying. Let the mind of God come crashing into your life and break off all of the other perspectives that rob you of the moment that you're standing in or the purpose that you are to fulfill. Give yourself to God in fasting and prayer and make history with Him there and watch how He uses your life as a weapon in His hand to affect history as you know it.

CHAPTER 13

AWAKEN THE NAZARITES!

"And the angel of the LORD appeared to him and said, 'The LORD is with you, O mighty man of valor!'"[149]

I remember when I first encountered the Lord, or I guess it would be better to say, when the Lord came looking for me and encountered me. My life was a total mess. By the age of twenty-one I was already heavily drug addicted, was drug dealing, was diseased—with a sexually transmitted disease that science still doesn't have any cure for—I found out I had herpes. I was

---

[149] Jdg 6:12, ESV

broken, violent, hopeless, and lost. In my mind and heart, I considered myself to be incredibly far from God.

Didn't grow up in church whatsoever. Didn't have Sunday school, kids church, youth group, nothing. My family life was broken early in my teenager years. Then my parents got a divorce. I was kicked out of my house and spent most of my teenage life living on the streets and out of my car.

I was kicked out of my house and spent most of my teenage life living on the streets and out of my car.

I got expelled from high school—that means that they thought the school would be a better place without me being there. I had a restraining order put against me for every school campus in the county that I lived. On top of all of that, I also had a restraining order put out against me for several of the nightclubs, Walmarts, and other locations in the part of the city that I lived.

Life was very chaotic for me. It wasn't heading anywhere positive, and I was doing everything that I could do to accelerate what was heading towards more destruction and eventually death.

I didn't know if God really existed or not. I didn't grow up in a Christian house and then just choose at some point that it wasn't for me and that I was going to do my own thing. I didn't know God, and I didn't really care to know Him at all. My life was one full of sorrow and great suffering.

I didn't understand much about my life and I coped with my reality by drowning myself in drugs, alcohol, and the pleasures that I could repeatedly give myself to. If there was a God, I was running one hundred miles an hour in the opposite direction from where He was. At least that's exactly what I thought.

I walked the streets at night completely wasted out of my mind on drugs, with tears streaming down my face, and I would regularly look up into the sky and say, "I don't know if You're real. I don't know if You, or who, is even out there. I have no idea what You're like, but if You are out there somewhere, You are the only one or thing that can get me out from where I am. I'm stuck here. I'm going to die here."

You see, I knew that I wanted to change, but I also recognized that I had been rendered powerless to produce the change that I knew I desired to happen in my life.

It was when I was running hard that I found myself, rather than running from God, running right into God.

It was when I was running hard that I found myself, rather than running from God, running right into God. There are many more details about my personal story in my first book, *Free Indeed: Free to a Life of Obedience.* I would encourage you to grab that, as it has some wild stuff in it that God did that is remarkable, and it is an overall healthy injection of fire to a heart that longs for Jesus. But I did, I ran right into God.

It was two weeks after my twenty-first birthday, at an altar in a church in Central Florida on a Sunday night, October 6, 2002. I saw Jesus in a vision. He completely wrecked my life, and I have never been the same. He instantly set me free from drug addiction, alcoholism, anger, rage, brokenness, lust and perversion, trauma, and more. I came out of that one encounter a brand-new man, a new creation. Praise God!

Jesus completely wrecked my life, and I have never been the same.

Now, I had been set free, but I still had to learn how to live in freedom; the two are not the same thing. Many times, we forfeit what God has done in the place of our freedom because we haven't yet learned to develop a consistency in living free. God can work it in in a moment, set you totally free in a second with one touch, one encounter, but then you have to learn how to walk out what God has worked in. The two are not the same. I had to learn how to live free, and God is faithful.

A few weeks after my encounter with the Lord I was baptized publicly. A few weeks after that I was gloriously filled with the Holy Spirit and the evidence of speaking in other tongues. And a few short weeks after that, in January of 2003, I received prayer during an altar time at the conclusion of a Sunday morning service after our pastor preached a message about God's desire to work miracles in our lives. I came to the altar and God did what no man can do.

I returned to the doctor and found out that the disease that once was a perpetrator in my bloodstream was nowhere to be found. The blood of Jesus gave me an answer that man has not found, science and doctors do not have, and money cannot buy. Praise God! I was a blazing ball of fire in those days. Well, and in these days too.

The Holy Spirit wildly encountered me through the night with dreams and visions of things that were to come.

My life had been completely wrecked and everything that I ever thought would happen to me took a wild 180-degree turn. I seemed to be shot out of a rocket, up and into God's purposes for my life.

The Holy Spirit wildly encountered me through the night with dreams and visions of things that were to come. Honestly, I didn't understand much of anything of this at all. I didn't ask for it. I didn't seek any of it whatsoever. I just wanted to love Jesus and to learn to love Him well. My life had been totally transformed and I was so deeply grateful to God that I just wanted to walk with Him.

It is amazing to see all God does when we give Him our yes.

Honestly, that was more than enough for me. But it wouldn't relent. Stadiums, massive outdoor gatherings, other nations, distant lands and people groups, churches small and large, prisoners set free, bodies healed, people's lives radically encountered and changed by the Holy Spirit for the glory of God. God's dreams and desires were unleashed into my heart and life and I was totally overwhelmed by it all.

We live in days of fulfillment now from things that God showed me back in those early days of my being born again. It is amazing to see all God does when we give Him our yes. He takes those that the world rejects and counts as weak and useless and raises them up to be instruments in the earth that display His mercy, grace, and power to the world around us. He takes those that nobody has ever heard of and the rest of the world would say doesn't have the qualifications and uses them to shake and change the world as we know it.

In other words, God doesn't look for what the rest of the world looks for. God doesn't seek man's opinion on who His selections should be. God has no problem whatsoever looking over everybody else that the world considers ready and worthy and snagging the older man who's been broken for decades on the backside of the wilderness.

He has no issue overlooking all of the strong and qualified to seek out the ruddy little faithful shepherd boy. It is a joy of His to call the tax collector and the zealous Pharisee. God does what He wants with whom He wants, and no one or nothing can stand in His way.

I am not sharing any of my story here with you to create some sort of résumé-building exercise where you think to yourself, "Wow, how special he must be." Actually, this would be the exact opposite of that. I am sharing bits and pieces of my personal story and journey with you so you can understand that God doesn't qualify us by our résumé.

God takes those who feel they don't have the right résumé and turns them into reformers, revolutionaries, and revivalists!

What your résumé in life may read right now is not what stands between you and a life that you may have always dreamed about in God. What stands in your way is the yes that God is looking for that you may not be willing to fully give over to Him. For if I have learned anything over my time in walking with God it is this: God takes those who feel they don't have the right résumé and turns them into reformers, revolutionaries, and revivalists! That's right. God takes your broken résumé, your accumulation of mishaps, failures, and chaos, and works them all together for good in His purposes!

In those early days I was gripped with a burning desire to see God move.

In those early days I was gripped with a burning desire to see God move. I spent hours in prayer and intercession. Whole days got swallowed up with God in the secret place. I burned to see God shake the nations. I honestly didn't really know if my prayers in that season were working towards anything, but there was a great sense of being overcome and sharing in the burden of the Lord for the harvest of every people, tribe, and tongue.

In those moments, I remember a prayer that came up often. It seemed to be an anthem for me. I would cry out, "God, I should be dead right now, but You kept me alive. Therefore I want this new life that You have given to me to count; make my life count! I want my life to matter! Use my life to make a difference!"

Now, I know that may sound cliché to you, but it wasn't to me. I hadn't ever considered such a thing before because the way that my life was going up until that point was surely going to have me dying on the streets, in a jail cell somewhere, or in a hospital bed. Those were the only foreseeable options that I felt I had. So, to now have this new life in Christ, to be filled with an overwhelming zeal that God could, and wanted, to do impossible things, was completely foreign to me.

But it didn't matter. I wasn't going to give in to any limitations in God. I had dealt with limitations my entire life and wasn't about to just adopt them in a different way now that I was walking with God. Some of us have limitations that we have conjured up and placed upon our lives that God has not intended us to carry. It is time to break off all of the lies and limitations in Jesus' name.

Some of us have limitations that we have conjured up and placed upon our lives that God has not intended us to carry.

I wanted my life to count. This isn't just the noble request of a young man with a cool testimony. This is the cry that the Holy Spirit births in our hearts. This is the jealous desire of God in our hearts that aches and longs for God to have His way, in us, and in the earth around us. This is a cry that acknowledges God wants to do something, and I want Him to use me to do it.

This isn't just for the transformed drug addict. It isn't just for those healed of incurable conditions. It is for every son and every daughter of God. It is for all of those who have caught a glimpse of this great King and now realize that for every breath that they may be granted to steward they will use it to honor Him and bring Him glory, wherever He may call, wherever He may say to go.

I burn now with a greater desire to give more of myself to Him than I have ever known.

I don't find it to be coincidental that in the days when my heart burned for my life to matter that the Holy Spirit drove me towards fasting and prayer. This was the way that God answered the cry He had put in my heart. The Holy Spirit invited me into ways that I could give more of myself over to God.

This is what people consider to be the honeymoon phase of walking with Jesus. Others who have been around for quite some time for some reason find some weird satisfaction in discouraging those who have newly seen Him and are burning afresh. "You'll calm down after a little while." "Don't worry, all of that will wear off in no time." All of the nonsense excuses for passion for Jesus always create a sense of heartbreak for me. It has now been almost twenty years and I am no better than I was in those beginning days. In fact, I burn now with a greater desire to give more of myself to Him than I have ever known.

Please don't ever give in to the lie that you have to calm down in the way that you love Him and go after Him. Please don't settle down. Please don't extinguish the flame that burns in your heart because you want to fit in with those who don't understand, or who don't want to understand. If you have been looking for someone and waiting for someone to give you permission to burn for Him and to go after Him in the way that your heart has always desired, this is it—don't be afraid of loving God too much.

I wanted to set myself apart for and unto God. I didn't know it at that time but what I cried out for was to live a consecrated life. Consecration is a word that we don't hear a lot about anymore. Consecration means to be dedicated unto something; it means to **Don't be afraid of loving God too much.** be completely given over for the service and worship of a deity. I wanted my life to be completely given over to God. Because of this covenant love that I was burning with I wanted to give my life to God and live a consecrated life.

This wasn't out of rules and regulations. It was out of being madly in love with Jesus and wildly possessed with God's Spirit. I had lived my life for everything else that there was out there in the world and I never was able to find the satisfaction and freedom that I had found in God. Why wouldn't I want to give my all to Him?

That was it for me. I was determined. My heart was set; it was all or nothing. I was either going to have all of God or it wasn't worth it to me. And knowing the desire in my heart, the Lord led me in beautiful ways into fasting and extended fasting. I didn't realize it at the time, but this was the way into everything that my heart had ever desired. I didn't realize it, but there was a Nazarite cry that was burning in my heart.

We can't live ordinary and then expect extraordinary to flow out of our lives.

A life of consecration and being wholly given over to God is something that we are familiar with throughout the Scriptures, especially in the lives of those the Bible refers to as Nazarites. Nazarites were a uniquely powerful people. Part of why Nazarites were unique and powerful is because their life and devotion was uncommon.

Nazarites were called to embrace what was uncommon and make it common to them. Nazarites were those that God invited into an abnormal lifestyle, so that He could do abnormal things. We can't live ordinary and then expect extraordinary to flow out of our lives. We can't blend in with the world and then expect the life of another world to be on display. Nazarites were a peculiar people.

When you study the word Nazarite, you find that it can be spelled two different ways: Nazarite or Nazirite. The reason is that the word has two Hebrew roots. One is the Hebrew word Nazar and the other is the Hebrew word Nazir. The difference in the spelling is obvious: one with the "a" and the other with the "i." However, though the spelling may be very similar, the meanings are actually quite different when you do the research.

Nazarite, which comes from Nazir, means, "set apart for God, sanctified, consecrated to reflect God's glory." The second Hebrew root word is Nazar, which has a similar meaning, "elevated above others, set apart, given authority over the land." When combined, the two Hebrew words speak of "being set apart, purified, being made to reflect the glory of God, raised above the norm and given authority over the nation."[150]

The term Nazarite is found in the Bible in Numbers chapter 6. There we find that anyone who desired to set themselves apart for God would have to embrace certain things as a part of their lifestyle. It was more

---

[150] John Mulinde, *Set Apart for God* (Sovereign World LTD, 2005), 71.

than just a verbal thing that you could communicate; you had to live it.

In Numbers chapter 6 it details it out this way, "Then the LORD spoke to Moses, saying, 'Speak to the children of Israel, and say to them: "When either a man or a woman consecrates an offering to take a vow of a Nazarite, to separate himself to the LORD, he shall separate himself from wine and similar drink; he shall drink neither vinegar made from wine nor vinegar made from similar drink; neither shall he drink any grape juice, nor eat fresh grapes or raisins. All the days of his separation he shall eat nothing that is produced by the grapevine, from seed to skin." ' "[151]

There are several other components of the Nazarite vow that they were to undertake as part of their separation to the Lord. All the days of your separation to the Lord there was to be no razor that could touch your head. There was to be no contact whatsoever with a dead body, for that would determine you to be unclean. All the days of his separation the Nazarite was to be considered holy as unto the Lord. [152]

You may be familiar with a few individuals in the Scriptures referred to as Nazarites. Samuel, Samson, and John the Baptist are the most obvious. All three men are released into the earth through supernatural

[151] Num 6:1-4, NKJV
[152] Num 6:5-8, NKJV

conception out of barrenness. There are angelic messengers to deliver words to parents about special purpose that would rest on their lives. One of these men is even filled with the Holy Spirit while in the womb!

For Samuel, Hannah makes her vow by saying, "O LORD of hosts, if You will indeed look on the affliction of Your maidservant and remember, and not forget Your maidservant, but will give Your maidservant a son, then I will give him to the LORD all the days of his life, and a razor shall never come on his head."[153] After this vow, Hannah gets a word from the Lord through Eli at the temple that shifts her barren situation. Samuel grows up in God's presence and becomes a powerful prophet and judge.

The angel of the Lord comes and delivers the word to Samson's parents about the baby boy that they are about to conceive, "Behold now, you are barren and have no children, but you shall conceive and give birth to a son. Now therefore, be careful not to drink wine or strong drink, nor eat anything unclean. For behold, you shall conceive and give birth to a son, and no razor shall come upon his head, for the boy shall be a Nazarite to God from the womb; and he shall begin to deliver Israel from the hands of the Philistines."[154] Samson becomes a powerful deliverer and judge.

---

[153] 1 Sam 1:11, NASB
[154] Jdg 13:3-5, NASB

John the Baptist has a similar introduction into the biblical narrative. The angel comes to Zacharias and declares to him, "Do not be afraid, Zacharias, for your petition has been heard, and your wife Elizabeth will bear you a son, and you will name him John. You will have joy and gladness, and many will rejoice at his birth. For he will be great in the sight of the Lord; and he will drink no wine or liquor, and he will be filled with the Holy Spirit while yet in his mother's womb. And he will turn many of the sons of Israel back to the Lord their God. It is he who will go as a forerunner before Him in the spirit and power of Elijah, to turn the hearts of the fathers back to the children, and the disobedient to the attitude of the righteous, so as to make ready a people prepared for the Lord."[155] John gives himself to God from his early days in the wilderness of fasting and prayer and appears as God's prophetic deliverer and judge.

Each of these men was born out of barrenness. Each of these men was delivered into the earth with signs and wonders and angelic messengers. Each of these men was determined from before their first breath that the rest of their life would be given over to God in a very special and powerful way. Each of the men we described was called and anointed for a

---

[155] Luke 1:13-17, NASB

specific task in their generation. The greatness of their call required them to enter into a great place of consecration. We must understand that great calling requires great consecration.

In light of all of this I want to draw your attention to something that we read over pretty quickly and may not have grasped as strongly as it is intended to be. There is something special that we read in Numbers that I

We must understand that great calling requires great consecration.

would like to point out to you. The verse in Numbers didn't say that it was only for those who were selected before they were born. The Nazarite vow was not for an exclusive group that only God would determine. No, it reads very different than that. It says, "When a man or woman wants to make a Nazarite vow...."[156] The word desire can be used interchangeably here for the word want, because in this context they share the same meaning. So, when exchanging want for desire it would read, "When a man or woman desires to make a Nazarite vow...."

Did you see it? The only prerequisite for giving yourself to God is desire! Oh boy, oh boy! All you need is a burning heart and a willingness to give yourself

---

[156] Num 6:2, NIV

over to God and you immediately meet the qualifications. It might have sounded difficult when we were talking about angelic messengers and supernatural birth deliveries, but now things have just gotten very practical and very real. You are no longer excluded, but you are included…if you have a desire to be!

When you completely abandon yourself to Him you find it all and you have it all.

What is in your heart? Do you have a longing for God that you just can't satisfy in worldly ways? Do you carry a sense of significance in your heart to see God break into the earth and do amazing things in your generation? If so, I would encourage you that you may carry a Nazarite cry and just haven't realized it yet.

You will never lose out by giving more of yourself to God. Consecration is not for those who are losers in this life, meaning we go without the things the world values and celebrates to just simply continue on empty-hearted. No, Jesus is our portion and He is our prize. The prize always outweighs the pain. When you completely abandon yourself to Him you find it all and you have it all.

The Nazarite vow is one founded upon desire. To all who are willing to come, come. To all who burn, come. To all who recognize the painful longing on the inside that just cannot be satisfied by anyone or anything else, come.

Man or woman, come. Young or old, come. Qualified or disqualified, come. One and all, if your heart is filled with desire and drawn into separating your life unto God, come. As it said, some would vow for short-term periods of time and others would hand over the rest of their lives.

What would it look like for you to prayerfully give more of yourself over to God? What ways has God already been speaking to your heart and drawing you into Himself that you have resisted because you didn't want to seem like that weirdo, or that radical Christian, or that extreme person?

This world is not your home, and we've got one shot to give it all in light of eternity and our love for Jesus!

I believe that there has been a tug upon your heart. I can say that confidently because I know that is what God does. He says, "Hey, that may taste good to you now, but come and taste and see that the Lord is good." Stop trying to satisfy your life with being what others consider to be normal. Stop living beneath your heart's desire to be fully given over to Him. Stop trying to fit into places that God never asked you to fit into. This world is not your home, and we've got one shot to give it all in light of eternity and our love for Jesus!

I believe God will grip your heart and bring you deeper into Himself and His purposes through a life of consecration with fasting and prayer. I am asking the Lord to burn a cry in your heart for a consecrated life that is fueled by His covenant love. Nothing weird, religious, and rule driven, but born from above in your heart and life by the fiery flames of loving devotion.

I believe God will grip your heart and bring you deeper into Himself and His purposes through a life of consecration with fasting and prayer.

May the Lord call you to shed the things of the world because of what you have found in Him. I am believing for extended times in fasting and prayer, and even forty-day fasts. The potential shaping of history has been given over to those who fast and pray. Will you join your life to God in fasting and prayer? Will you enter into the secret place with the Lord and contend for cities to be turned upside down, nations to be shaken, awakening to come to continents, the face of Jesus to be revealed in your generation? The Lord is looking, but who will He find?

Determine what your vow will be to the Lord. Will it be short term? Seasonal? The rest of your life?

I wanted my life to count, and I have found the way that it does. I have found my significance in the secret place with God. Abandon all of the other pursuits that will soon fade away. We are living for eternal rewards, not earthly applause...or at least we are supposed to be.

Beloved, it is time to give your life to God; history is depending on you. Give your life fully to God in fasting and prayer and watch Him turn your life into a weapon. May consecrated lovers arise in our day and become weapons of mass destruction to the enemy's plans. May consecrated lovers arise in our day and become agents of deliverance and fulfillment unto the desires of God. It's time. He is worthy of such a people!

Michael Dow

Michael Dow and his wife, Anna, have been married for thirteen years and they have four children together. Their family resides in Orlando, FL, where they lead a growing group of house churches called The Father's House. He is the cofounder and president of Burning Ones, an international ministry team helping people all over the world experience the love and power of Jesus and live more passionately devoted to Him. Michael is the author of several books, including *Fasting: Rediscovering the Ancient Pathways*. Michael holds an undergraduate degree in theology from Southeastern University in Lakeland, FL, and travels the world preaching the Gospel with powerful signs and wonders following into gatherings of all kinds.

STAY CONNECTED TO MICHAEL DOW

 @michaeldow

/michaelsdow

 @michaeldow

BECOME A PARTNER

BURNING ONES IS HELPING PEOPLE AROUND THE WORLD
EXPERIENCE THE LOVE AND POWER OF JESUS AND LIVE
PASSIONATELY DEVOTED TO HIM.

FOR MORE INFORMATION ON BECOMING A PARTNER
SCAN THE QR CODE BELOW OR VISIT:

BURNINGONES.ORG/DONATE

DOWNLOAD THE BURNING ONES APP
STAY UP TO DATE WITH ALL BURNING ONES NEWS

In the app you will have access to messages, worship,
news and updates, the Bible, livestream events, and much more.

RESOURCES

FOR OTHER BOOKS, RESOURCES, AND MERCHANDISE
SCAN THE QR CODE BELOW TO VISIT THE
BURNING ONES ONLINE STORE.

CONNECT

CONNECT WITH BURNING ONES

@_burningones

@burningonesinternational

www.youtube.com/burningones

Info@BurningOnes.org

Burning Ones
PO Box 772610
Orlando, FL 32877